Sales Decoded

5 steps to 'Powerful Selling'

Amit Sharma
Lakshmi Sirisha

Powered by

24by7publishing.com

The book "**Sales Decoded**" is self-published by the author.
All the printing & distribution process is powered by
24by7 Publishing
13 New Road, Kolkata - 51, India
http://www.24by7Publishing.com
Contact@24by7Publishing.com
+91 9831 470 133

ISBN: 978-93-84882-87-7

MRP: INR 375.00
Version 1.00

Powered by

24by7Publishing.com

Dedication

Dedicated to Our beloved

Guru Ji

SAINT. DR. GURMEET
RAM RAHIM SINGH JI INSAN

About the Authors

Amit Sharma is currently heading Dishah Strategic Solutions (www.dishahconsultants.com) business consulting company as the CEO. He has over a decade long experience in heading sales initiatives at various levels from frontline sales to Executive Management.

Contact him at: amit@dishahconsultants.com
Linkedin :https://in.linkedin.com/in/amitsharma04

Lakshmi Sirisha works as Lead Consultant in a reputed IT MNC. She has over a decade of experience in business process and strategic consulting. Her expertise spans across multiple domains handling high profile & strategic Accounts and million dollar deals. An MPhil in Computer Sciences, Lakshmi Sirisha is an avid book reader; a voracious speaker involved in several state level public speaking events and has been awarded with several accolades

Preface

PEOPLE BUY INTO THE LEADER BEFORE THEY BUY INTO THEIR VISION.

—John Maxwell

I know one great leader

Steve Jobs was a young entrepreneur building Apple in the 80's and the board of Apple wanted an 'adult' with business experience to come in and run Apple instead. Jobs met John Sculley who at that time was the president of Pepsi and sealed the deal for him to onboard and run Apple by saying these famous words

"Do you want to sell sugar water for the rest of your life or do you want to come with me and change the world?"

In this little yet very famous story, what do you think moved Sculley to risk his very successful career and accept the offer?

Could Scully see the future?

Has Scully got sold on Steve Jobs simplicity and charisma?

No, Sculley got sold because he was presented with a very challenging opportunity that had a great potential Sculley always wished for.

If you carefully observe the statement, Steve, managed to demonstrate how well he understood his own goal, his target audience and their requirement. Steve did the following:

1. Steve knew that Scully is a successful executive and would love exploring challenges of greater potential.

2. Steve skillfully underrated Scully's current task at hand by calling it 'Sugar Water'
3. Steve pitched his offer by positioning it as the greatest challenge and opportunity at the same time by phrasing it as 'change the world' which any successful top level executive will wish for.

Steve had precisely figured it out that Sculley liked bigger challenges with greater potential and he carefully orchestrated his sale pitch to Sculley and won him over to join Apple. And, this proves, why Steve Jobs is also known to be the best Sales Leader in the world.

Yes, to be a great sales leader you should know the art of pitching because success of selling doesn't lie in a successful product or a successful company but in 'Successful Pitching'. And learning the art of 'pitching' can get you whatever you wish for – Career, Success, and Dreams turning into reality. Wondering how?

We are in a social world that is globalized. We have people involved in anything and everything we do or don't do. It starts with family, friends, classmates, colleagues, customers etc… Every minute we deal with people in personal, social and professional space and require them to believe in and support us to fulfill our dreams. An entrepreneur requires pitching his ideas to investors/Customers to gain support, guidance and Success. A Sales Leader requires pitching his products to customers, partners for success. A student needs to pitch his projects to school, college management for support, guidance and exposure.

Yes, to be successful, you are required to successfully pitch your dreams, ideas, ideology etc… So, sales pitch exists everywhere in our world – like the air we breathe. However, very few people make use of it to its fullest potential and get themselves separated from the rest to become leaders who can sell their dreams, products, ideas or vision to anyone.

Learning the art of successful selling is not as easy as it sounds. Sales pitch is a demonstration of how good you understand your target audience, their personal or business needs, your idea or product, your market space, your own organization and your competitors.

During the course of this book, we will learn different components that affect your sales pitch like prospect business, his Needs, your product, market space, competitors, Sale Operation, Sale Process, Selling Skills etc… and how these can be used together to customize and design your sale pitch and be a winner.

I aim to create leaders

In a decade long successful sales career, we have trained a lot of Sales Professionals and students from technical and non-technical background, in field and online sales. We have seen Sales Rep encountering multiple challenges related to Engaging Prospects, Building Pipeline, Handling Big and Strategic account, Sales conversions, getting bigger investments on first orders etc…

In due course of learning and experimenting, we have understood the core challenges that hinder Sales Reps growth in winning an account at its true potential and strategies & techniques that successful sales leaders have employed to overcome these challenges.

This book is focused on bringing these techniques that so far has been used by industry Sales Leaders to every Sales Rep that will transform him into a Sales Leader that the industry desperately needs. A leader, who is capable of winning all types of small, big or strategic accounts at its true potential and thus winning big investments and mind share of prospects,.

This book aims to create sales leaders of tomorrow. Leader who:

- ❖ Knows how to take strategic approach to selling.
- ❖ Equipped in winning accounts of all sizes including the high potential, big ticket deals
- ❖ Equipped in steering strategic accounts and partnerships successfully for their company
- ❖ Focused in brining revenue and customer insights for product / market developments and innovations
- ❖ Equipped in increasing mind share through relationship building and thought leadership
- ❖ Handle any customer meetings - face2face, online presentation, Roadshows, Public Speaking etc…

In short, we aim to create Sales Leaders of tomorrow.

This book is written with a single goal in mind to decode the art of selling through learning about your prospects and creating successful sales approach used across the entire customer lifecycle. It takes a scientific approach designed after years of research and practice to create winning sale approach for meeting, Calls, presentations, webinars and closing the opportunity. So, let's begin the journey to master the art of selling.

How to study this book

The book is focused on thoroughly discussing the components of Sales Pitch/Approach as a science. Book revolves around discussing Strategies, Tactics and activities one should adopt to transform himself as a complete sales leader. Readers are requested to:

1. Study each component as a practice.

Each of the component discussed in the book thoroughly discussed to stress the importance of the component in the sales pitch, what is expected of a sales rep, prospect's psychology during each of the phase and what does he expects from his sales rep. Hence, each component is a practice in itself and readers are requested to treat it as an exercise.

2. Involve the activities in your Sales Approach

Each of the activity discussed in the above section should be performed by involving it into your sales approach before moving on to the next one. This would ensure that each of the components is practiced thoroughly and understood. A step by step approach would be more suitable here to take the complete advantage of the book and the practices discussed.

To make the most of the book, do not forget to download the free resources provided towards the end of the book that will play a crucial role in effectively implementing sales approach mentioned in the book.

Amit Sharma & Lakshmi Sirisha
April 2016

Acknowledgements

Mr. Virbhan Sharma, Ms. SnehLata, Ms. Radha Rani & Mr. Manmohan Sharma, thanks for having faith in us.

Sumit, Sri Harsha Tadepalli, Brijesh Pradhan, Manju Sharma & folks at Dishah, appreciate your unconditional support and valuable inputs.

Tanmay for being the little wonder you are.

All the Sale Leaders of the world, thanks for being our inspiration; and for constantly reminding the business world that great strategies alone may not bring growth but great sales men will certainly do.

Examples, stories, anecdotes shared in the book are gathered from various sources like Newspapers, Magazines, and Presentations.

We have made a sincere effort to acknowledge the sources referred. Regardless of the source, I wish to express my gratitude to those who may have contributed to this work, even though anonymously.

If inadvertently we have omitted giving credit, future publications will give due credit to those that are brought to the author's attention.

Index

Sales Landscape and Challenges

Sales has become challenging

Before we dive deep into learning Sales Pitch and its components, it is quite important to understand how Sales Landscape has changed in this information age due to emergence of Internet, globalization, Social Media and cut-throat competition.

With the emergence of Internet, Social Media and various other online channels available today, everything has changed about buyers, sellers, sales process and decision making.

Buyers prefer to buy online

Buying is rapidly transitioning from offline to online. In this e-commerce era, buyers can buy anything and everything online including personal and official things, properties, property registrations, utility bills and the list goes on. As such buyers prefer to buy online.

Role of information in decision making

Buyers now depend on two things to make their decisions about a vendor. Amount of quality information available online about products they wish to purchase and reviews and feedback available in public space like social media or public forums that can be used to form an opinion about the product and the vendor.

What are its implications?

a. Buyers prefer online engagement. As a result, offline or field sales are contracting to in-house sales and this is the future.

b. Buyers would like to engage with vendor whenever they wish for it and not when the vendor wants it.

c. Buyers are much more informed about the product specifications, reviews and have already formed the opinion about the product. They also totally understand their precise requirements. This makes it difficult for sale reps to convince prospects by sharing basic knowledge about the product.

d. Buyers wish to make right decisions. Buyers seek extensive knowledge about the product, its benefits, use cases, implications, additional requirements, value for the money invested. In short, they expect their sales rep to be an advisor, an expert guiding them in making right decision by sharing more and more information that extend beyond the boundaries of solution features. They want their advisor to help them explore territories like solution benefits in terms of revenue and profit and how it makes their business competitive.

World economy, business dependency and its impact on Sales

Multiple Decision makers

With the last economic crunch the world has seen, there has been a lot more change in B2B buying process then B2C buying process.

Now, even smaller purchases involve multiple key decision makers from various departments. This has made buying decision complicated. It has become difficult for sales reps to bring all the decision makers together in one room, call or meeting unless a closing decision is required or there is an urgency of the solution for the prospect.

Easy access to competitor products

With the growing competition, prospects awareness of competitive space and importance of online selling, your competitor is just a call/click away and this is posing a lot more challenge for vendors and Sales Reps to engage and retain prospects and customers by being proactive otherwise your prospect/customer will become your competitor's customer is no time.

Buyer's quest for more information

Buyers are now much more informed with their buying decision. This trend has resulted in buyers expecting more in-depth information from their Sales Rep. Don't worry I have got good news as well. This trend also has a positive impact on sales process. Sales cycles have become shorter and for good Sales Rep, it has become easy to establish rapport and trust with prospects to convert them to buyer by sharing more and more relevant information and acting as a trusted advisor.

Sales Rep Challenges

Changing Sales Landscape is posing multiple challenges for Sales Reps at every stage of the sales cycle. Now that we have a feel of the wildness of this jungle, let us see what kind of challenges it is posing for Sales Reps that needs to be overcome before we can learn the art of converting a cold prospect into a buying customer.

Changing Buyer behavior

The first challenge, information age is posing, is the ever increasing information quest of prospects for right decision making at every stage of the decision cycle. A simple sales process of sharing information about product features, benefits and implementation challenges have completely changed to learning about vendor reputation and history, competitive advantage that it holds, Unique Value that it has to offer, Business Stability, Future Plans, Customer Success stories have become a regular part of the game. This is amplified by having multiple decision makers involved in buying decision. This has made is difficult for Sales Rep to not only engage the buyers by earning their trust but to meet their expectations as well. This has also made the negotiations complex like never before.

Sales Management challenges

Sales Reps are plagued with decreasing territories and increasing sale targets. And, this phenomenon is ever increasing as businesses aim for higher growth. This is amplified by the cut throat competition they have been facing. They have been facing tough competition not only from their direct competitors selling similar solutions but also from other indirect competitors who are competing with them for prospect's time and money in general. This is making tough for Sales Reps to get appointments from prospect out of their busy schedules.

With the advent of online marketing and disappearing line between sales and marketing, Sales Rep time and energy is lost between highly productive and less productive accounts. This is amplified by ever increasing sales funnel leaks at all stages.

What hasn't changed yet and still crucial?

All Prospects are not the same

Prospects today do have ever increasing expectations but still all prospects do not have same requirement, same priorities, same growth plan, and same buying capacity. Totally driven by their business size and goals, not all prospects have same requirements. In short, not all prospects are the same.

Customer Experience and Vendor Professionalism

Customer experience (CX) is the quality of interaction between an organization and a customer over the duration of their relationship. This interaction includes a customer's attraction, awareness, discovery, cultivation, advocacy and purchase and use of a service. Customer Experience today is the driving factor for businesses and corporates to engage and retain customers. In internet era, anything that doesn't go well with customer experience or related to vendor professionalism can turn off the prospect and shift him to your competition with just a click. Buyers have also been more vocal about it due to the emergence of Social Media. This allows buyers to share their experiences and thoughts about Vendor professionalism in the public space.

Business Relationship

Prospects are becoming more informed on products and companies through more and more information available in public space likes Social Media. An informed prospect now seeks a trusted advisor to guide them through the decision making process. They need someone who can be trusted with handholding in making a business decision that will result in current and future gain for prospects. As such, relationship with prospects in selling process still holds the utmost importance.

Business ecosystem and Sales

There has been humungous growth in startups in this information age. Every company wants to grow from their existing space and reach out to next space like startups wish to become mid-size organizations or corporates. This push from the bottom of the funnel has a growing wave effect in the mid-size business segment as well as corporate segment. This has resulted in adding an emotional component to B2B selling. Prospect expect a lot from the solution and this has a 360 degree impact on sales. Prospect expect an inexpensive solution with far reaching current and future benefits while keeping the cost of maintenance low.

Recommendations and Referrals

Recommendations and word-of-mouth still matters to a business to gain momentum and have a greater impact at every stage of the sales cycle. Recommendations convert a cold prospect to a hot qualified lead, a qualified lead to an engaged prospect and from an engaged prospect to a customer.

So, my friend the route is not easy but one thing for sure is that the solution to all these challenges are directly or indirectly connected to sales approach you take to handle your accounts and once you have mastered the art of sales approach, these won't be a worry as you would put yourself on the winning path of greater and better conversions and meeting and exceeding your quotas beyond expectations.

Prepare to be a LEADER

Remember the story of eagle rebirth.If not – here it is - Eagles extend their lifespans by going through a painful transition of breaking and tearing apart their beaks, talons, and feathers in order to grow new ones. Yes, every transition is painful and requires a great amount of focus, dedication and continuity in efforts.

To be a great sales leader requires a great amount of commitment. Yes, I am not going to lie to you. Every Sales Leader you see today have gone through this and it is not easy in the context that it would require dedicated and continuous efforts every day before you fully transition to a sales leader that can get involved in sale account of any size or importance, any sale or marketing discussion, any presentation online or offline in roadshows, seminars etc.

In short, this transition would require you to

- ➢ Develop the right 'Attitude'
- ➢ Building perfect 'Customer Persona'
- ➢ Mastering the 'Sales Process'
- ➢ Building the 'Winning Sales Pitch'
- ➢ Becoming a Complete 'Leader'

These are the components that design your winning sales approach that puts you on the path of sales leadership to crack any account and situation and convert BIGGER and BETTER.

In the due course of the book, we will study each of the above listed components, role played by the sales rep, prospects psychology, expectations and complexities attached.

The winning attitude

Once a bird asked a Bee, after a continuous hard-work, you prepare the honey. But a man steals the honey. Do you not feel sad? Then the Bee replied: Never… Because a man can only steal my honey not the art of making honey..!!

The winner's edge is not in a gifted birth, a high IQ, or in talent. The winner's edge is all in the attitude. Attitude is the criterion for success. — Dennis Waitley

A positive attitude can make whole lot of difference between a winner and a loser. Complementing it is the 'Right Approach' that can reduce the distance to success. To be a sales leader, you must adopt a right attitude and approach. Below are the 8 golden rules that will help you learn and adopt the right attitude and approach that is needed to be a leader in this new sales world.

Believe in what you sell.

Yes, you have to be convinced with what you are selling. Unless you understand the value your solution offers to your prospects or the difference it can make to them or their business, your prospect won't believe in you or your solution. I have witnessed numerous encounters with Sales Rep who talk about their product by the script with no understanding of its purpose; the end result is they struggle to convert accounts and meet their quotas. They are never sure of what they are selling because they never believed in its potential. This is not the attitude of a real Sales Leader.

Your belief in your product makes a lot of difference to the way you describe it to your prospects. We are humans and we go by the emotions exhibited on face, in voice, body language and hence regardless of the channel you take to communicate, we only understand emotions and if the emotions and belief is missing, your knowledge is as good as dead. A Sales Rep who believes in what he sells, is enthusiastic about his solution gets a lot more attention and trust from the prospect. So, believe in what you sell.

Be the first to reach the customer

As per a recent survey in sales space, 55% of time, a prospect is likely to a buy a solution from a Sales Rep that approaches him first. Well, that figure can really turn your conversions upside down. Furthermore, prospectsthat enquire about a solution and get a contact within 1 to 2 hours are likely to stay active and buy from the same Sales Rep.

Love to talk to strangers

Why it is needed?

People enjoy conversation with other people. A prospectwould also like to make a pleasant conversation, would like people to listen to him, understand and empathize with his business challenges. This makes an emotional bond and help breaks the ice between the two and setup a bridge to share each other problems, questions, feedback and what not.

We see Sales Rep who usually are monotonous and makeprospect feels that early he gets out of the conversation, the better it is.

Now, that is the death of business relationship and will never lead to a sale. Instead, it creates a wall between the prospect and Sales Rep that he would never prefer to cross.

What wonders it can do for you?

I had a friend who championed this art of breaking ice with prospect in minutes. The result is, prospect go out of their way to

share information (sometimes confidential information as well) like competitor's quote, how your solution and your competitor's solution is being perceived internally by decision makers, questions that are going to be asked to vendors in the next meeting and what not. And he used this information to all his advantage to do more and more conversions. Yes, he is that good at it.

So, breaking ice with prospects can do wonders and has an unrealized potential of winning or losing the deal.

How to master it?

There are multiple simple ways that you can take but nothing can be as significant as asking someone about his day with genuine interest. Yes, that opens up people straight away plus gives you a feel of the kind of mood he is in and can very well help you set the momentum of the conversation.

What are exceptions to it?

There are prospects who usually are in hurry or who are not over friendly or friendly at all. Well, there are exceptions to everything but nothing wrong in being nice to them and asking them about their day. Some people would like to get information first before they open up. This is a very rare case but if you don't find it to be working with them, it is always safe to come to the point straight away without wasting any time. Eventually, after receiving the information, they will open up.

Interest to know your prospects

I was working with this Sales Rep who used to handle big and strategic accounts for his firm. Every time I see him on phone or in a face to face conversation with his prospect, he would discuss prospect's personal interests. He knew his prospects to an extent that he could discuss soaring real estate prices in one of the city of California while sitting in India. He does this by researching prospects personal interests through every source he has access to and uses it to his advantage to get prospect attention. He curiously asks questions about prospects interests in sports or other such activities and uses that to build conversation.

This bonding is the first step to building rapport and trust. A Sales Rep who invests in learning their prospect's interest will always come out as a winner. Remember once you have prospect's trust, he will confide in you to share any kind of information you need and will trust you to buy your solution.

Have a problem solving attitude

Yes, a prospect approaches a Sales Rep with a problem expecting a solution to their problems. How would you feel when you are just offered a blunt 'No, we can't do it" as an answer to your problem. This goes deeper into his memories and will always stop him from approaching that vendor again. This can be a definite end to a relationship even before it begins.

What if you can be given an alternative to your problem or being guided to another solution or location for the problem? Wouldn't you feel nice and connected and would remember this gesture for a long time? According to a survey done recently, 35% of times prospects will buy alternatives suggested by the Sales Rep,since they value the expert advice offered as highly professional.This will not only gets you future business but also help you gain the mind share. With an increased mind share, you can expect future gains as well from the same prospect.

Now, one would argue as to why we should suggest alternatives that we don't have. Yes, it might not bring an immediate gain for you but it will bring an immediate mind share for your company and its service. This gesture will convert into trust and prospects would be more than happy to reach out to you 'first' whenever they would need something that you have to offer. Plus, they will be more than happy to mention and refer you among their community which will again bring more tangible and intangible gains for you.

Treat every prospect equally

I knew this Sales Rep, who was very enthusiastic, and can attract prospects and talk about their problems and solutions he has to offer and everything was perfect with him till the point prospect mentioned his requirements. If the requirements are limited or potentially small, unknowingly he will let out an impression of "Oh no, this is a petty requirement" and make prospect feel uneasy. Does this ever happen to you as well when you had any requirement and you approached a vendor? I bet many a times and you would have felt bad as well.

This is dubbed as a deal killer just because you didn't know how to be nice to prospects with limited requirements. Instead, you are supposed to respect the fact that prospect is interested to bet his money on your solution regardless of however smaller the deal size is. Your salary comes from his pocket! This attitude will not only help you gain a successful deal but also the mind share of the prospect which could turn into big profits in future. A Prospect whose current requirements are limited in size doesn't mean that it doesn't have a big deal potential in future.

Every win is a team effort

I knew this Sales Rep who was great at relationship building. He used to build relationship in every function/department of the company and with all the key people. What good that did to him? Well, a lot more than you could imagine!

With this relationship building, he could get the prototype of the solution built overnight for prospects regardless of the size of the deal. He could also expedite quotes/discounts approval with a ring of a phone call. That has always helped him gain an edge over everyone.

Additionally, everybody recognized his efforts and many a times, this used to be a topic at every coffee table during breaks. Well, it's like every day every key person would hear his name once. And you know what it means. But how he used to manage it?

By acknowledging every participant in the sale cycle, and maintaining a rapport. Every sale is a team effort – much more significant in mid-size and big deals solution selling. Every function has a part to play in the sale and successful execution of each part results in a successful deal. This requires every Sales Rep to appreciate the fact and share the credit with each function.

Yes, everyone needs motivation and what can be a better motivation than appreciation. As a Sales Rep, you should respect this fact and share the credit with everyone involved regardless of the size of the contribution.

Don't sell to someone who doesn't need

This is an energy sucker for any Sales Rep and a complete waste of time for him and his prospect. I know in an effort to meet or exceed your quota, Sales Rep try to reach out to prospects that might have a need but you are not sure of. Well, no harm in giving a try to assess his/her needs but once you have an idea that he does not have an immediate need for your solution, step back to save yourself huge amount of efforts and time. You cannot get a penny out of the pocket of someone who doesn't need your olution.

Know your CUSTOMER (KYC)

A disappointed salesman of Coca Cola returns from his Middle East assignment. A friend asked, "Why weren't you successful with the Arabs?"

The salesman explained, "When I got posted in the Middle East, I was very confident that I would make a good sales pitch as Cola is virtually unknown there. But, I had a problem; I didn't know to speak Arabic. So, I planned to convey the message through three posters.

First poster: A man lying in the hot desert sand...totally exhausted and fainting.

Second poster: The man is drinking our Cola.

Third poster: Our man is now totally refreshed.

And then these posters were pasted all over the place.

"Then that should have worked!" said the friend. "The hell it should had", said the salesman.

"Didn't realize that Arabs read from right to left"

What do you think would have happened next?

A simple story to describe how important it is to know your prospects.

Knowing your prospect is all about understanding his business including details like business model, business portfolio, business goals, business customers etc. These are discussed in details below.

Prospect's Business Intel

A shepherd was tending his flock in a field, when a new sports car screeched to a stop on the road nearby in a cloud of dust. The driver, a young man in expensive designer clothes and sunglasses, leans out of the window and shouts over to the shepherd, "If I tell you exactly how many sheep you have here, can I take one?"

The shepherd looks up slowly up at the young man, then looks at his peaceful flock, and calmly answers, "Sure, why not?"

The young man steps out of his car holding a state-of-the-art palmtop PDA, with which he proceeds to connect to a series of websites, first calling up satellite navigation system to pinpoint his location, then keying in the location to generate an ultra-high resolution picture of the field. After emailing the photo to an image processing facility, the processed data is returned, which he then feeds into an online database, and enters the parameters for a report. Within another few seconds a miniature printer in the car produces a full color report containing several pages of analysis and results. The young man studies the data for a few more seconds and returns to the shepherd.

"You have exactly one-thousand five-hundred and eighty-six sheep, including three rams, and seven-hundred and twenty-two lambs."

"That's right," says the shepherd, mildly impressed. "Well, I guess that means you get to take one of my sheep."

The young man makes his choice and loads the animal onto the back seat of his car, at which the shepherd says, almost as an afterthought, "Hey there, if I can tell you what your business is, will you give me back my sheep?"

The young man, feeling confident, agrees.

"You're a consultant," says the shepherd.

"Wow, that's right," says the young man, taken aback, "How did you guess that?"

"No guessing required," answers the shepherd, "You showed up here even though nobody called you. You took a fee for giving me an answer that I already know, to a question I never asked, and you know NOTHING ABOUT MY BUSINESS. Now give me back my dog."

In short, prospect Business details or information is quite crucial for any Sales Rep to understand the current state of the business. If you are not aware of prospect business, you might never estimate or understand his challenges and pitch him a right solution at the right price. There are innumerable benefits to understanding prospect business. Let us understand why it is important for a Sales Rep to have a complete idea of prospect business and his challenges.

Why do you need his business Intel

Customer Program

Every organization sells their products and services in packages created and optimized based on their customer business and requirements. Each package differs in terms or core offering and/or additional benefits. A Sales Rep core responsibility is to recommend an appropriate 'Customer Program' based on prospect requirements. He is there to understand prospect requirement and recommend him the appropriate solution. Every company has separate Customer Program for different types of customers like for Resellers, Distributors, wholesalers and consumers. Learning about prospect business in the initial phase of the interaction can help you recommend the right solution to the prospect and also establishes you as an expert in front of your prospect.

Missing to gather the right prospect business information will lead to serious problem like recommending incorrect solution in the beginning and later on switching to right solution which results in prospect losing trust, extended sales cycle, difficulty in account conversion and/ reduced ticket size.

Rapport building to simplify decision making

Earning 'Prospect Confidence' in the beginning of the sale conversation is very important for a Sales Rep and if not done properly, it can result in prospect losing interest and turning off the conversation with you or the company itself. But how do you establish connect with the Prospect? Every prospect wants to talk to someone who is an authority who can quickly understand his business and challenges and recommend a solution that completely fits his requirement. In short, simplify the decision making for him. When a Sales Rep manages to gain prospect trust and confidence, it does wonder as prospect gains a solution that is a complete fit for his requirements and will be ready to pay more for it and Sales Rep gets prospect trust and convinces him to invest more.

To be seen as an authority to the prospects, Sales Rep should try to understand prospect business model and offering and using that information Sales Rep can help connect with the prospect better to gain his confidence.

Up-Selling and Cross-Selling Multiple Products

Most of the companies include multiple Products and Services in their portfolio and majority of the products are targeted to the same industry vertical. Understanding and knowing prospect business presents a great opportunity to sell multiple products at the same time or recommend him your products for future consideration at the time of selling. In the beginning of the interactions, this keep the prospect interested as many of their requirements can be met by one single vendor. This further strengthens your chances of winning the account and that too at a larger ticket size.

Exploring 'Strategic Partnership' Opportunities

Yes, conversation opens up multiple avenues of business and one of them includes strategic partnerships. Strategic Partnerships are ones where two business entities come together in a partnership to harness multiple opportunities presented by partnership. There are innumerable numbers of partnerships like promoting each other product, sharing assets, product integrations etc…

Sales Rep being the frontrunner for the company can help discover these strategic partnership avenues with the prospects by having a deep understanding of his business.

What Business Intel Count?

A prospect is trying to solve his business challenge through your solution. For this he approaches a Sales Rep to discuss a solution. A business challenge and your solution combined includes multiple aspects that a Sales Rep needs to be completely aware of that will put him in a situation where he exercise a complete control over the sales account and its course.

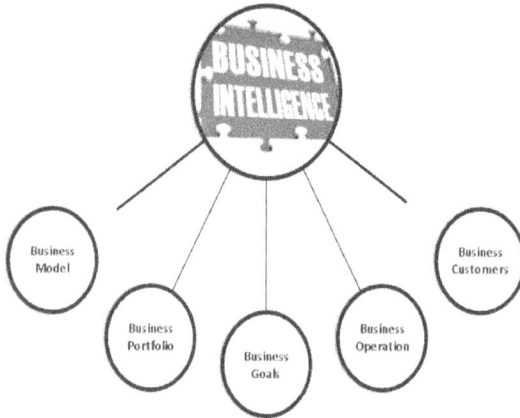

Gathering prospect business information is a great asset for any Sales Rep and does wonders for him.

But the question remains as to what type of information a Sales Rep needs to gather that will prove substantial in deciding the sales approach such that he can win maximum accounts at their true potentials and stand out from the competition as a winner.

Let's take a look at each aspect closely.

Business Model

In terms of business space, Business model refers to how an actual product or solution is packaged & delivered for its target audience. In general, businesses can be classified as:

B2B (Business to Business): This is quite important to learn if the prospect or account you are dealing with is a business and if he is a business then what type of business is it? There are businesses that act as a channel and further resell your product or service to consumer (B2B2C) by either just reselling or value added reselling. The best example of this would be computer 'System Integrators' and 'Hardware Resellers'. System Integrators offer computer hardware with added values in form of assembled systems and/or warranty and/or extended support. Hence, these are also called as Value Added Reseller (VARs).

However, Resellers are pure play reseller and they just sell you the hardware without any value adds. A Best example of this kind of model is mobile stores that just resell the mobile phones and accessories without adding any value to it like extended support or stuff like that. You might have to contact the vendor also called the Original Equipment Manufacturer (OEM in short) for the support. For a bird eye view of types of business, check the below categories:

Depending upon nature of business, a business may sell directly to consumers or choose to add a link or two as channel for targeting consumers.

How does this helps?

Your business model might have variations in itself and might have a different solution and/or different business model altogether for different types of business customers. This information will help a Sales Rep understand the nature of their prospect business and recommend the best suited model based on their requirements.

Since, every business caters to his audience based on the business model. Direct consumers of the product or service you are selling will have different requirement and challenges whereas as a channel partner business, your needs, expectations and challenges would be quite different from the direct consumer. Hence, it is quite crucial for a Sales Rep to understand his prospect's business model.

Business Portfolio

Products and Services offered by your prospect as part of their business portfolio is a great insight. It can unlock multiple opportunities for a Sales Rep for upselling and cross selling.

Upselling is a sales technique whereby a Sales Rep identifies prospect needs and recommends more expensive items, upgrades or other add-ons for the same core solution in an attempt to meet prospects current and future requirements. It also makes a more profitable sale for Sales Rep. While it usually involves selling or marketing (in case of no urgent need) more profitable services or products, it can be simply exposing the prospect to other options that were perhaps not considered by him.

Cross-selling is the practice of selling an additional product or service line. In practice, businesses define cross-selling in many different ways. Elements that might influence the definition include the size of the business, the industry sector it operates within and the financial motivations of those required to define the term.

In this information age, this information is accessible from business website and can be used to your advantage for upselling and cross selling.

Business Goals

Business goals are what a business is looking to achieve inshort and long term. Business goals in generalcan reveal information on business current and future requirement. This can open gates to multiple opportunities like:

1. Prospect current and future requirements might extend to the new features or a totally new product that is currently under-development and hence can help you position your product as the complete fit for prospect's current and future requirements and will help you position your brand above your competition.

2. Current and Future requirements might open the avenues of Upselling. Yes, if you have approached prospect to sell your datacenter services and you get to know that he is pushing for automation in Sales as well. Boom! You can aim for housing of their CRM Server as well.

3. It also opens avenue for cross selling. You have come to sell your call center solution to prospect. Probing into his business goals have revealed that prospect is aiming for higher level automation in Sales. Great! You can now easily pitch for your new CRM solution that you have just launched.

Business Goals are a great indicator for prospect's future requirements. However, it is quite surprising that Sales Reps restrict themselves with no interest in learning prospect's business goals.

Business Customers

It is crucial to know your prospect's Targetaudience particularly if they are B2B type; who are a business in itself and offering products/services to another set of customers. Target customers (also called as target audience in marketing language), are the actual customers a firm is aiming to sell their products and services. This can be the same as the industry itself or a sub-set of the industry.

Your prospect and his target audience can be similar, or different. A very good example of this would be: your prospects are telecom industries like Airtel, Vodafone etc... However, Vodafone and Airtels' target audience includes all types of consumers who need a phone.

Understanding prospect's customer space and industry offer great insight and value to a Sales Rep in multiple ways. Let's take a look:

Identify prospect's key requirements

A prospect needs your solution to solve a business challenge. Your solution might be the part of your prospect's business model that will help them serve their clients better by offering exceptional services. However, a Sales Rep who doesn't quite understand their prospect's target audience will not be able to understand how prospect's customers are using the service and will not be able to describe how his prospect and their target audience will benefit from using his solution. A good example of this is, centralized AC Chillers. A centralized AC used in big malls, hospitals etc…

Business (A): AC Chillers Supplier

Business (B): Construction Builder

Business (C): Builder's Target Customer

Business(A) is a centralized AC Chiller supplier who supply centralized chillers to construction builders (B). Construction Builder (B) uses centralized chillers in constructions of Hotels, Malls, Hospitals, and Research Laboratories etc… symbolized as Customer (C).

Requirement of AC chiller specifications differs from Malls to Research Laboratories and so no. A Research Laboratory may require precise temperature handling which might not be the case for Mall or a Hotel. Hence, without knowing the exact requirement of Customer (C) for an AC chiller, a Sales Rep might not be able to pitch the right features of his solution to construction builder (B) and might end up losing the deal just because of the lack of Customer (C) exact requirement. Hence, a Sales Rep should have a complete knowledge of his prospect's target audience (C) exact requirement before pitching his solution to the prospect.

Rapport and Relationship Building

Having knowledge of your prospects target audience can help a Sales Rep position himself as knowledgeable and trust worthy in front of his prospect. Prospects love to have know-how of their target customers industry. Who doesn't? This is why they are in business and any discussion, information, or an expert advice on industry trends, pricing trends, sales and marketing trends will interest them and this in turn help a Sales Rep establish himself as a trusted advisor before his prospect on whom they can rely for proper understanding of their requirements and suggest a solution that is a fit. It also opens avenue of upselling, cross selling and strategic partnerships with the prospects wherever possible.

Business Operation

A Water Purifier Sales Rep is approached by admin of a school who needed replacement for 4 water purifiers. Sales Rep provided him with the pricing details along with a quote. However, Admin was looking for more discounts and a better deal which was beyond Sales Rep limits and he was put across to the Manager.

Manager entered the scene and started inquiring about prospects requirement of water purifier. Manager made an offer but kept inquiring about their business and requirements. After rounds of questions and discussions, manager derived the following information from the prospect:

1. Their current requirement is of 4 water purifiers.

2. They have a total of 12 water purifiers in the school and remaining 8 would be up for replacement in about 3 to 6 months.

3. There are 4 branches of the school in the city and over 20 branches across the country.

4. Their current contract is from City level supplier.

Manager sensed a big opportunity and with the help of the admin team member tried approaching other admin teams and the key decision maker to nail down a country level contract with the school by offering a better deal and service to all the branches of the school.

The result: a couple of thousand dollar deal suddenly turned into half-a-million dollar contract. Much bigger margins for the Sales Rep and not mention the kind of praise and reputation it would bring to the Rep and the organization.

Every sales rep realizes how important it is to know his prospects current requirements and purchase potential. If a Sales Rep can estimate the correct potential of his prospect then that helps a lot to define the sales approach for the account and identify stakeholders and their level of involvement.

If a prospect ishavinga potentialofbig investment thenyou might involve your manager and sometimes vice president as well whereas other accounts have limited involvement of your manager based on the account expected size. But how many times do we get it right? At what stage? These are the key questions that need to be answered. An account cannot be won at its true potential unless the potential is identified at the very beginning of the discussion. But how do you do it?

The best indicator to identify an accounts true current and future potential is learning about prospect's operation and its size. Size of the operation not only indicate the current and future requirement trends but it also helps you identify following key information:

Prospect Business Challenges

Yes, the depth of prospect challenges and business requirements can also be assessed from the size of business operation. Size of prospect business Operation can be measured through multiple metrics that would depend upon the information a Sales Rep would like to draw. In general terms, for a quick understanding, operation size can be measured through number of offices and branches across a city, country or globally. It can also be measured in terms of number of employees the company has etc… It would solely depend upon the type of solution you are selling.

A great example of this is: if you are a computer sales rep then you would like to understand the number of machines prospect has it its office, how many offices are there in total etc…

In sales domain, this is a great opportunity to understand the types of requirements and challenges prospect can foresee.

Business opportunities

It also opens avenue for cross selling. A big operation involves multiple assets management. This creates an opportunity for salesreps to assess and upsell/cross sell multiple solutions andservices.

A Sales Rep involved in selling website services, visits his prospect that is looking to upgrade his business website. While taking about prospect's operation size, sales rep identifies that they are also in need of digital marketing services. Great! You can now easily pitch for "Digital Marketing Services" as well that will get you more investments than website building services.

Once a Sales Rep has understood his prospects, he can then build their persona that will help him address his prospect requirements precisely. After building the 'Customer Persona', he can then craft his winning sales approach for each type of prospects that he handles. This would be quite useful when having interaction with his prospects.

Customer persona helps you assess:

a. What are the key requirements of your prospect?

b. What are his current challenges and what would be his future challenges and requirements?

c. What would be the size of his first order and how frequently he would do repeat purchases?

d. What are the key features and benefits that he would find appealing?

e. What are the motivators to drive him across the sales decision curve?

Based on "Customer Persona", a Sales Rep can decide the best Sales Pitch that your prospect would find appealing and interesting that would enable him to pursue your solution and invest in it. An example of customer persona categories is provided further below.

Customer Persona

Below is the typical customer personas built after researching on the associated attributes. However, the customer persona is not limited to these categories and can be built as per individual business requirements. For the book purpose, we have highlighted typical categories that are general in nature and serve as a great platform for any Sales Rep regardless of the industry he belongs to.

Customer persona can be built for two types of customers viz Direct Customers and Channel Partners (Reseller, Wholesaler, and Distributor)

1. Direct Customers
    a. Current High Potential

      b. Limited Current Potential but future high potential

      c. Limited Potential

      d. Strategic Partnership

2. Resellers and Distributors

      a. Current High Potential

      b. Current Limited Potential but future high potential

      c. Limited Potential

      d. Strategic Partnership

Each of the sub category mentioned above has separate business challenges/needs and require a different sales pitch to convert these accounts better for new and repetitive business revenue. The primary reasons for varying potential are operation size, business goals, type of customers served by the business etc... This is discussed in details in coming sections.

Hence, each category needs to be targeted with a separate sales pitch as well as approach and has different requirements and objections before these can be converted successfully. Before we could craft a winning sales approach for each category, we need to draw their persona using the attributes mentioned below. Let's take a look at these attributes.

1. Business Information
2. Challenges
3. Needs/Wants
4. Action Drivers
5. Potential Purchase Size
6. Sales Cycle & Period
7. Concerns and Objections

REVERSE ENGINEERING Approach to KYC

In traditional approach, to build a customer persona, first attributes are gathered about prospects like his business type, operation size, requirements, potential etc… and then a customer persona is built out of it. However, in contemporary 'REVERSE ENGINEERING' approach, first we take a customer persona and start identifying the associated attributes. This is quick and very effective approach.

REVERSE ENGINEERING approach is more suitable in situations where a company has existing customers and insights from existing customers is used to build 'Customer Persona'.

Tip

In situations where a company is a startup and no customer database is available, 'Bottoms Up' approach is more suitable. In bottoms up approach, we start identifying the attributes as and when prospects interactions are handled to build customer persona. As more and more interactions are handled, enough insight will be available for a Sales Rep to build customer persona.

Know your PRODUCT

Product or Service knowledge forms the basis of any selling process. Without having the complete knowledge of your product or service you will find yourself wandering in the dark or always dependent on your technical team for software and/complex products or solution designing.

However, learning only the features of the product doesn't work either. Sales Rep should know all aspects of the product which includes FAB (Features, Advantages and Benefits).

Did it ever happen to you that you see yourself dependent on technical teams for product demos, solution building etc...?

Did you experience that prospects handled by your technical team becomes inactive or decides to go for competition solution?

This happens because of the simple reason that each decision maker involved in the buying process comes from a different function, having different priorities. Hence, the same pitch for all decision makers is not going to work. A simple example of this is, if you are selling a solution to a decision maker who is a CEO and expects a solution to solve his bigger problems of generating revenue, or automation, or productivity etc...however if your technical team talks about the product performance or technical dependency or the technical specification, this would end up in turning off the prospect instead of making him happy.

Here, our goal is pretty simple; we want to understand:

1. How our products features and advantages are prioritize by different decision makers

2. What kind of keyword and language do they use to describe their requirements? This is important because you do not want to use keywords that are new to your audience and confuse them.

Hence, a product has to be understood by a Sales Rep from different buyers perspective so he can co-ordinate meetings and be in the driver seat to prepare pitch for the solution according to buyer requirements while his technical team takes a back seat in giving a pure play technical assistance to his Sales Rep.

Types of Decision Makers

We are going to study in the chapter as to various types of decision makers involved in the buying decision, their priorities & challenges and what your sales approach should be to win them over. To understand the approach, we need to understand the type of decision makers involved first.

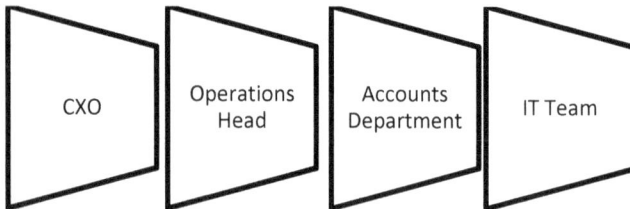

Executive decision makers – CXO, President, VP or director level

Management people look at solution to address bigger challenges for them. Challenges that relates to the below quickly gets them interested and connected with the sales rep. Hence your product features and benefits to be highlighted are ones that addresses the bigger challenges.

a. Revenue,
b. Profit
c. Automation
d. Productivity
e. Brand Building

Hence, you should be discussing product features and benefits that links to the above category as well as share details like

1. Product Cost over its lifetime
2. Other associated cost
3. ROI
4. Break even

To understand this, let's take an example of AUDI car that is designed for Executive Level Professionals. Noticed their sale pitch is all about the looks, performance and status symbol.

Now, do you think an executive level guy coming to Audi store would be interested in hearing how comfortable the car is or how inexpensive it is compared to other cars in the same space? He will not. Hence, pitching comfort and price would be completely irrelevant here.

It is important that you tag each features benefits and advantages based on the above categories and use these as part of your pitch during calls, meetings and presentations.

Operation Heads

These people are the ones who are the actual users of the product. Being a user of the product, they would be interested in:

1. Simplicity to use
2. Features offered that make their everyday task easy
3. Additional support like product manuals, online or onsite training to train their new and existing staff on its usagebased on the complexity of the product.

Hence, a Sales Rep should tag features and benefits of the product based on the above categories and use them when pitching solutions during product demos, webinars and presentation accordingly.

Accounts department

These are the people who only understand the money language. They are more interested in:

5. Product Cost
6. Purchase Procedure
7. Renewal Procedure
8. Invoice

Hence, talking to them even about the product features would be a complete waste of time for you and for them as well. Instead, they would like to understand the cost and saving part of buying your product and should be dealt accordingly.

IT Team

IT team is the one that maintains company's IT affairs like IT hardware, software management. They are only bothered about the product deployment and management. Hence, these people are more interested in learning about:

1. Hardware and Software requirement of your solution if any.
2. Specification and performance.
3. License Management of your solution.
4. Renewal, upgrade and migration of your solution.

Hence, your product pitch should focus around these features and advantages and not on the core functionalities of the solution. This would keep them interested when they are listening to you.

So, we have seen how priorities and expectations for a solution changes with every type of decision makers. Let us understand how to gather this Intel.

Decision Maker's Intel

Data comes from use cases of existing customers. Existing customers offer a lot more insight that can be used to solve all your problems related to insight on

1. Building Customer Persona
2. Prospect needs
3. Prospect usage model
4. Market space and Competitor knowledge

During the course of this book we would also learn how to segregate this information from existing customers to build your perfect approach for each type of prospects/account/projects you handle.

To understand how our product features are perceived by each type of decision makers, we would need to interact with the following resources:

1. Existing Customer Database

2. Existing Customers presales tickets
3. Sales Reps handling existing customer's accounts in case, it is separately handled by your firm.

FAB – Features, Advantages & Benefits

While travelling on my way back home from the office, I noticed an advertisement for iPhone 5c. It had a beautiful 'nature' picture with a tag line written at the bottom saying 'Shot on iPhone 5c". Wow. This is the one thing that would come out of your mouth when you would see the picture. This was enough for the ad to grab anybody attention. But what is the point I am trying to make here. Check out the tag line – it doesn't talk about:

1. How high resolution camera it has or
2. How easy it is to take a picture.

It just highlights the quality of the picture to the finer details because that is the top level requirement/challenge for iPhone customers. Their primary usage of iPhone is for clicking pictures and everybody wish to have a clearer picture. So, the ad talks about the result and not the feature itself.

Yes, prospect expects to solve a challenge or meet an expectation and that is the value he is looking in the solution to deliver. But how do we find out that. How do we associate each of the features available in the product? This is done by building the insight into the prospect primary usage of the features and draw current challenges. This is the next important component of the winning sales pitch and has multiple implementations in sales cycle. We would start by how this insight is used to create value. It starts with:

F⌐	A⌐	B⌐
Features	Advantages	Benefits

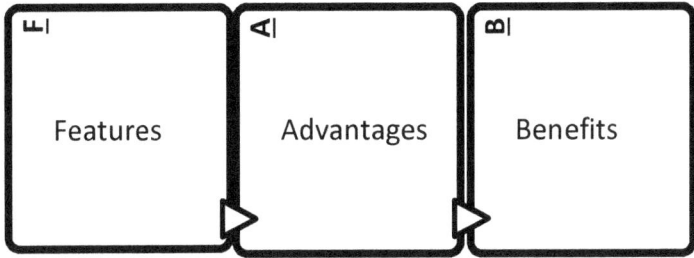

Assessing Prospect's needs

A feature can be highlighted in multiple ways. Like in the above case, I can highlight ease of use of the camera, or I can highlight shake proof images etc... but what is going to fly among the target audience will be decided by the following factors:

1. Primary usage of the feature
2. Magnitude of the challenge they face

To understand this, a Sales Rep requires closely studying and understanding the business model of the target audience. This requires you to study:

Customer's product usage

Is your product used/consumed by the end user for themselves or it is being resold to end users. This is quite an important step because a Sales Rep needs to understand how the product is being consumed and by whom – especially in the B2B market space. This would give you an idea on how the product is being consumed and what functionality holds importance in that case.

To explain this, I would give you an example of Mobile Phone:

Mobile Phones for Professionals and college students:

Mobile Phonesare being used by business professionals. To a business professional, work related features are more important like email integrations, office integrations and stuff like that. Hence, they would be more interested in learning about these kinds of features and how the phone would make their life easy.

However, college students are the ones that would be interested in pictures, music, movies and stuff like that. They won't be interested in emails, office stuff as that would be completely irrelevant to them.

Hence, it is quite important for a Sales Rep to understand their target audience and their business model and to ensure that you pitch the right solution to the right audience with the right pitch.

In case, your customers are a channel and re-selling your solution to other end users then you should understand their customer's business model and needs. If a customer is purchasing aMobile Phone from you is a reseller and would like to resell the Mobile Phone further to the end user then you should know who his end users are like professionals or college goers and accordingly pitch your solution to him to increase your chances for conversion.

Remember, our aim is to identify the needs of our target audience and select the features that address their needs and requirements.

Market Intelligence

This is the quiet an important step in becoming an expert Sales Rep. Market Intelligence or Industry knowledge refers to how in general people is using your or your competitor solution or other similar solutions. This insight can then be shared with the prospects which will help him discover multiple use of the solution and you would be positioned by him as a trusted advisor with great amount of knowledge. This holds more importance in cases where your prospect is looking to start a new business or service and would totally depend upon you for insight in product usage by end users.

To give you an example, iPhone for college students is being used for movies, music and photos. Now, you have noticed many students' inquiries to you or on social sites and forums about iPhone Application integrations for Jobs seekers. This is a great insight and would be very useful for college students. Hence, while talking about movies, music and photos, you can also talk about how they can seek jobs, send applications, create audio/video resume copies and contact HRs. This is an additional and very important insight for them and they would love this coming from you.

Hence, it is quite important to gather insight on additional uses of your solution for specific target audience that add value for them and would make you a trusted advisor.

For B2B selling

This holds a great importance in B2B business space where customers/channel partners would be very interested to know how other customers are using the solution, packaging the solution, pricing and marketing the solution. Hence, it is recommended in B2B selling that you should gather this information.

Gather market Intel

There are multiple resources to be used to gather insight on prospect business and industry. The best place to start with is researching on the existing customers. You can segment existing customers based on product usage and then research on how the product is being packaged, priced and used for. Research could include calls, face to face meetings or browsing their website.

Next best resources would be internal sales team handling existing accounts including sales team manager, management people who could not only share insight on target audience but also on industry and market space.

Put Market Intel into action

This is important – we need insight and not just information. Hence, as a first step you should gather all information on different customer segments based on product usage.

Once you have prepared the segments, you should understand how the product is being consumed to address the type of requirements and challenges. Then, you should prepare the list of top features based on the need and associate value to it based on the usage.

As a next step, you should add priority to the features so that these can be communicated during calls, presentations etc in the order of priority. As a thumb of rule, you should remember the top three features and value associated to hook up prospects without any support or assistance from any of resources or tools.

Know your COMPETITION

Do you feel helpless when prospects talk about your competitor product and you end up saying ' I don't know about their product, but this is how you can use our product' or even worse ' let me connect you to someone who can help you with this question' or ' let me arrange a call back from my supervisor'.

This creates an adverse effect about your reputation and turn off the prospect because he wants to know how you compare yourself with the competitor and what best you have to offer. This is the time when you should be most prepared and show that you are way above your competitor in everything you do including the market and industry awareness you have.

Yes, the biggest challenge for Sales Reps in today's information age is – positioning yourself above your competition to win the mind shares during the sales interaction. Why this is a biggest challenge, it's simple; competitor information is available on internet all the time without any prior contact and prospects have access to it to make up their mind.

However, this presents a very good opportunity as well if you can make use of this information to work for you. But how do you do it? To understand this, we should first understand what prospect wants to know from a Sales Rep about the competition.

Prospect wants to know a couple of things like:

1. How better your product can help him than competition?
2. How better your product is priced compared to competition?

3. What additional valuedo you have to offer him compared to competition?

Everything discussed above boils down to the following:

1. Features and value offered by you and your competition
2. Know what features are missing and the difference in value
3. How competition has packaged the product?
4. How competition has priced the product?
5. What is their USPs?

This is the primary information that is easily available that you can grab and consume to face prospect questions and sound ready as ever. However, this information will only help you to encounter prospect questions. But how do you position yourself above the competition. This is done by highlighting their weakness in areas what matters most to prospects and makes a whole lot of difference to him and his business.

Value Proposition	Business Reputation	Training & Support	Customer Focus

These areas are:

1. Value delivered by the features
2. Overall business reputation of both the vendor and competition
3. Additional services offered like support and training
4. What is their customer focus – same as yours or different

This proves to be great insight for you and should be used in your sales pitch to highlight the difference between you and your competition. Let us understand each of the points carefully.

Identify 'Value Proposition'

This is a feature by feature comparison between your solution and your competition solution for the value delivered across the prospect needs and wants. For this, as a sales rep, you should have a complete knowledge of what features and value delivered by your competitor solution.

You would require creating a customer persona of competitor product – just like your product, across features and weighing the value for each feature. This step would help you understand how you stack up against the competition in features and value delivered plus helps you explain it to the prospect to highlight the weakness in value delivered for any one or all features.

Mark 'Business Reputation'

Everybody wants to be associated with a brand that is highly reputed in terms of solution offering and complete satisfaction to the customer. With this idea in mind prospect compares multiple similar brands to understand the differentiation offered by them and which one is more suitable for their business needs and more reliable.

Since, it is a direct comparison between the brands that prospect seeks, it is quite obvious he would raise related questions to understand your brand position compared to competition. How can you overcome this?

Thiscanbedonebyunderstanding whereyour competition is lagging in terms of solution offering and/or support offering. This insight can be gathered by visiting competitor's support forums, blogs section and social media accounts to understand what prospects and customers are complaining about. Once you have gathered this information, you can use it in your sales pitch when encountering questions related to comparison between brands. You can highlight the complaints about the features and value, pricing, customer support, commitments, trainings etc.

This would help you place yourself right above your competition in your prospect mind and will prove vital in establishing you as a trusted advisor.

Study 'Support & Training' infra

Many solutions today are very similar in nature and different in terms of support and training offered by vendors. Hence, it is quite important that you should understand support services and training programs offered by your competition. Some vendors offer paid support, others offer online support, some offer offsite support. This can be very big deciding factors for prospect especially in cases of complex solution deployment and hence it can help you rate yourself above the competition and win the deal.

Customer Focus

Apple and Samsung offer similar phones however, their focus of audience is completely different. Apple wish to target the audience that can afford to pay $700 or more for a phone but that is not the case with Samsung. Samsung focus is on the phone desirable to anybody looking to buy a phone below $700.

A Sales Rep should be aware of this comparison and should highlight it as a positive point to uphold his brand. A simple thumb of rule to identify this comparison is the price. However, it can sometimes get complicated and extend to other attributes as well.

Really good Sales Rep, even keep an eye out and keep assessing and predicting competition next move such that it can be highlighted as part of the discussion. This includes, finding out next set of features as part of the upgrade they will release, or promotion they are planning in the coming quarter or a new product they have been coming out; with that Sales Rep can use it to their advantage.

This can be done by continually studying their competitor's customer support forums, blogs and social media sites where during customer support, a technical support person will highlight the features they are planning as part of the next release based on customer questions or concerns for existing bugs and stuff like that.

This gives an edge to the Sales Rep to be really in the driving seat of the sale discussion.

This bring us to the close of the preparedness discussion which will help you understand the components of a sale pitch and how you can lead to establish yourself as a trusted leader in front of the prospects and help him establish his confidence in you and your solution right from the beginning. Let us now move forward and understand how and where you would need to use your sale pitch and how to modify it for each stage of discussion and for each situation.

Gathering business information can be general as well as specific to a particular business or industry. For the sake of the book, we have highlighted the general information that needs to be gathered about prospect business. This information applies to all types of business verticals and horizontals.

In addition to the information provided here, sales reps are advised to gather details which are specific to their business or industry as well.

However, while framing your questions for prospects to gather inputs for his requirements, we should remember that the prospect business can be a consumer, retailer, and distributor based on product usage. Hence, we should accordingly draft our questions. In case, a consumer is an individual and product is a commodity like a shaver then these questions might not be a complete fit and should be modified according to the goals of aSales Rep.

Master the SALES PROCESS

Sales process and sales pitch go hand in hand. Every stage of the sales process is unique and includes a set of activities to be performed to move your prospect down the sales funnel. In this section, we will have a detailed study of what makes a sales stage, activities included and how you can enhance your sales pitch to win more deals.

But before we explore each stage of the sales process, what is crucial about it and how you can leverage skills to master each stage; we need to first understand the sales process stages highlighted below for your reference.

A sales process stage varies from 4 to 10 depending upon individual sales cycle of a product or services. However, in a nutshell, any sales process includes the following major stages that can be further broken down as needed.

Prospecting & Qualification

Meeting/Presentation/Webinar

Product Trial

Quotes/Negotiations

Closing

Each stage has its own set of activities and its own set of challenges. Understanding and overcoming the challenges will result in prospect advancing further down the funnel.

Prospecting & Qualification

- Do you face a lot of rejections in your prospecting or qualification calls?

- Do you really feel a fear of rejection when you call someone you don't know? Or

- Do you see prospects not responding approvingly when you speak to them?

If yes, then this all relates to one common problem and that is - your sales pitch is not convincing enough to bind a prospect into a conversation with you.

The goal of "Prospecting & Qualification" stage is to earn a prospect and/or turn a cold prospect into a hot prospect and move him into the next stage of the process called "Presentation". In this stage of the sales process, you search and identify a prospect and connect with him using various communication mediums like phone/email/drop in to his office. This is the first stage of the sales process and primarily the deciding factor if you can make the prospect interested in your solution or not.

This stage has two parts:

Cold Call

In this stage, identified prospect is NOT expecting a contact from you. It requires you to browse and collect information about prospect, his requirements and connect with him to discuss the solution. This stage is quite difficult as you would be approaching those whose business requirements are not clearly known to you.

Warm Call

In this stage, prospect has made enquiry with you over a medium like website or phone and expects to hear from you. You also have an idea about prospects requirement and preference of the solution through enquiry forms or email or phone call etc.

This is relatively easier than Cold Callas it confirms prospect interest of your solution as well as give you access to his email or phone or time to engage him.

Prospecting & Qualification Challenges

"Prospecting and Qualification" stage has its own set of unique challenges. This stage is the hardest part of the entire sales process as you would be approaching or talking to someone you don't know about and explaining him a solution that he might not know about or hardly have an idea of.

a. Rejections: Rejections has been the major trend of 2015 in Prospecting and it will continue to be on the top in 2016 as well. Rejections from prospects are higher across consumers as well as business buyers segments. Sales Reps manage to reachthe right decision makers but still face rejections regardless of trying different approaches and pitches and this continues to hit their quotas badly. This is the most crucial step for pipeline building and continued rejections will have the effect on the Top Line.

b. Reviving buyer's engagement: Well, this continues to be another challenge for sales reps involved in demand generation. An initial effort does build up their pipeline but then keeping the buyer engaged and interested is posing a big challenge for sales reps. Prospects are busy and always running on tight schedule. Efforts are required to keep him engaged and active till the account has been pushed further down the Demand generation Funnel.

c. Prospect Profiling: This is the third biggest challenge for the Sales Reps in the Demand Generation Funnel. Profiling a prospect requires understanding of his needs, buying potential, timings, solutions or bunch of solution that will fit his requirements. With the growing business portfolios; this is going to be a continued challenge for a Sales Rep to profile a prospect with the most accurate information that will help him in Prospect Engagement to convert accounts at their true potential and identify current and future business expansion opportunities.

These are the top rated challenges that Sales Reps will continue to face and overcoming these challenges will need you to strategize and plan your approach and sales pitch such that each hurdle can be crossed with minimum restrain and maximum output thus leading to conversions beyond expectations.

Well, like every big problem presents a bigger opportunity; if you can make your mark during the early discussions with the prospects, you will end up sealing the deal most of the time. Yes, a great impression here will ease your and your team's effort rest of the way. On the flip side of it, if you are failing to make a mark here, you might have a tough time convincing your prospect or worse he might not even give you a second chance. So, to solve this puzzle, we need to first understand what motivates a prospect to continue with the engagement and be interested in a solution that you are proposing.

Prospect's Experience Cycle

To solve this puzzle, we need to understand prospect's mindset when he searches for a solution; lands on your Desk or you search for a prospect and try to contact him. Prospect goes through a specific cycle as described below before he makes a choice and purchase a solution.

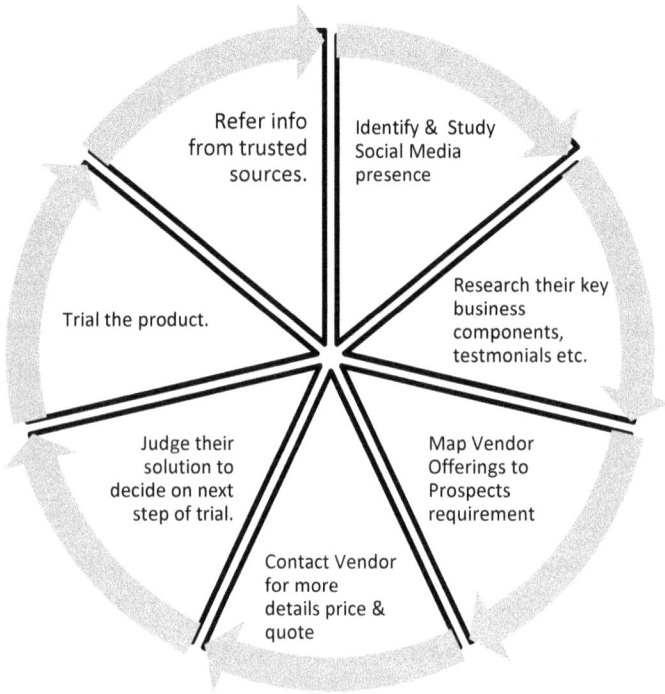

Prospect connects with vendors to understand their solutions and find a fit for their requirements. In today's global world, prospects are using internet to search for solutions. They connect with multiple vendors who are just a click away to understand their solutions. During this entire process, one thing continuously flows across the cycle and that very thing is the "Trust".

Prospects are wary of their purchase decisions in a new solution. This is even more complicated for cold prospects who are been approached by sales reps. It is significant in mid-size and large size purchase decisions and particularly "Products" that are not easy to replace. So, you can say the more the amount of investment involved in the solution, the more the trust factor is required and more time it takes for a sales rep to establish trust and thereby convert an account into a purchase account at their true potential. So, the final equation is:

'**Investment**' is directly proportional to '**Trust**' which is directly proportional to '**Sales Cycle**'

Trust factor requirement is higher at two places in the sales cycle:

a.   During the Prospecting & Qualification stage

During this stage, prospect is unaware and unsure of the vendor and the proposed solution unless you are Microsoft. He is also in fact, unsure of the Sales rep he is talking to. Hence, sales reps face a lot of rejections from the prospects. The rejections faced are more at the first contact. These situations can be salvaged by the only way of establishing "Trust". Yes, at this stage, a great amount of trust needs to be established by sales rep to convince a prospect and have proposed solution considered by prospect for his requirements.

b.   During the Purchase decision stage

In this stage, Prospect is ready to buy-in the product. Hence, he wants to make sure that investment in the solution is justifiable and vendor selected for this investment is trustworthy. This situation can also be salvaged by establishing trust in the solution and the sales rep. While mainly the trust here is driven by how the solution has performed during its testing followed by trust established by Sales Rep. However, in consumer and particularly in service industry, Trust is primarily driven by Sales Rep followed by the solution offered. It does have an exception for the exceptionally popular brands that are the market leaders.

We are first going to look into the "Prospecting & Qualification" stage and how the trust factor plays and how you can use it in your sales pitch to convince prospect to come for meeting or try your solution. This will help your prospects to confide in you and your solution. It will also help you to overcome rejections and convert more prospects to hot prospects in less span of time.

Trust

I recently went out to purchase my winter jackets. I browsed few good shops where Sales Rep helped me select one, patiently answered my queries but none seem to take me to a point where I feel comfortable buying an expensive winter jacket. The reason being none of them earned my trust that they understand my requirement thoroughly and can help my way out.

At last, I approached this shop where I met a Sales Rep who was through with what I am expecting and what I need. He tried to understand that why I need a winter jacket, what countries will I be travelling, what temperature I am expecting. He did share a good bit of information on how hostile a weather can be and what I can do to protect myself. The end result is he earned my complete trust and I ended up buying multiple accessories from him along with my winter jacket.

Did you see what wonder a simple 'Trust' can do to your conversion? Yes, you can not only seal a deal with trust building, in fact, you can have your prospect buy additional stuff through up-sell & cross-sell and he would be happy to not only buy from you but also to recommend you to others.

But my friend, Trust is hard to get and easy to lose but not impossible. After years of research and practice, I am listing down best practices that will help you build rapport with the prospects such that they completely confide in you and see you as a brand that can be trusted to buy solution from you. With this, you can have anybody confide in you within minutes of conversation such that you will be unforgettable to your prospects.

Let us understand what factors effects trust and how you can build it.

What makes a person trustworthy brand?

As per a research, a prospect takes about 7 seconds to frame his opinion about a person he is dealing with and more likely than not, it is not favorable. The first impression actually lays the foundation of the trust which is then evaluated and re-evaluated over time by prospects during the sales cycle till he makes his purchase.

To give an example, if you are on time for a meeting with a prospect or you have informed your prospect prior to walking into his office or setup a call time prior to making a call; this makes him feel that you are a professional even before he has seen you or interacted with you and made him think that you are serious about business. Whereas on skipping the schedule in upcoming meetings would make him evaluate and re-evaluate his initial impression and this time it would not be a good one for your personal and business brand.

There are a lot of things that creates a first impression which includes controllable and uncontrollable factors like your website and lot other stuff but in this book we will discuss the controllable factors, mannerism and skills one should acquire to create a first impression that converts into trust and helps a Sales Rep win a deal.

Regardless of the number of strategies and tactics one can employ to build initial rapport and trust, majority of it can be categorized in these three key factors that one must consider to build a trust that converts into results.

1. Personal Presentation
2. Solution Attributes
3. Prospect Attributes

What you see is what you believe. And first impression is the last impression. Yes, a prospect meets a Sales Rep before his encounter with the product. What I am trying to say here is that personal attributes matters a lot in sales and this is true for all kind of selling whether it is field selling or inside sales. It is a human nature that we try to make an impression of a person when we first meet him. I bet you also do it every time you see a new face. Everyone does it. And then we try to evaluate and re-evaluate our judgment about the first impression as we more and more interact with the person.

Business world is just like that. The only difference being, we become more skeptical in judging a person than in personal space. So, what makes your first impression count and form the stepping stone of building a relationship and trust.

Communication

Communication forms an eternal part of engaging with clients and has a key role in personal and business development. Without good communication skills, we cannot convenience anybody whether he is our boss, colleagues, HR, prospects or even family members. Yes, how you communicate your ideas will play a crucial role in how you are seen as a brand by your prospect. Great leaders and Sales Rep are known for how they communicate their ideas.

Communication is an important skill to gain if you wish to succeed in sales.

a. Etiquettes
b. Listening Skills
c. Interpersonal Skills

However, my purpose of highlighting communication here as part of trust building is not to talk about listening and talking skills. Instead, I wanted to highlight how communication affects your brand and how it can be used for brand building as a first step towards trust building.

A professional with good communication is highly regarded. Good or rather great communication is about matching frequency with the person you are communicating with, giving him space to share his thoughts with you and at the same time making him feel that he is being heard and comprehended. It is a difficult mix to achieve. However, following tips will keep you on track.

a. Prospect Interest first: When you have got a problem and you have come across someone who might be able to solve it, what would you like to do first. Tell him your problem and give him an idea of what do you feel about it or would you like to listen to what he has to offer. Yes, your prospect got a problem and needs an ear first before a helping hand. Unless you give him a space to speak out, you are not going to be even close to being into his good books. Overexcited Sales Rep tends to over talk about their solutions so much that they overlook prospect interest. Allow prospects to speak. This not only will make them feel comfortable talking to you, it's also a good technique to gather more information about their challenges and gain the insight which can be used to match with what your solution has to offer - features and advantages. This makes prospect feels he is being heard and at the same time keeps the conversation relevant and valuable.

b. Fast-Talking: Do you feel like when you have an opportunity to talk about your solution, you talk about everything that you know? This is bad in two ways. Everything that your product has to offer might be relevant to the prospect and his needs but the timing to mention it might not be right and relevant to the pain point being discussed. Yes, prospect might not be able to take everything at once and you might end up confusing him about your solution positioning and relevance. Secondly, while taking fast, prospect might get distracted and tends to miss the important details. This doesn't make any prospect enthusiastic. This should be avoided at all cost; after all slow and steady wins the race.

Talking too fast doesn't make you sound an experienced or an authority over a subject. In fact, this is perceived as nervousness of a person and can be seen as a deal killer.

c. Using fillers: This is another communication mistake that everybody tend to make at one or the other point by using fillers in colloquial speech patterns. We inject our words with fillers like 'Like', 'So', 'um', 'ah'. Initially, they seem so innocent but if used in the majority of the speech, they would take over your speech and makes it monotonous and less interesting to the listener. Your listeners will feel disconnected and bored.

d. Rambling: This is just another 'interest killer' and this happens all the time in phone as well as 'face to face' conversations. Rambling is not providing a short and concise answer to a question. It is in fact, perceived as an act of nervousness. For example, if your prospects ask you about the price of a product and you end up explaining him the entire pricing model without giving him hint of your product price will turn him off.These tips when followed makes conversation interesting and help speaker develop a favorable rapport with listener and help him being perceived as an experienced Sales Rep which is must for building initial rapport and Trust.

Conversation Hackers for trust building

Trust building completely relies on how you present yourself to a prospect. This includes from your dressing styles to your conversation mannerisms that creates a professional or non-professional image of yours in prospects mind. Use the below conversation hacks to build rapport and trust with prospects to create a lasting positive personal brand of yours and come out as a winner. These are well researched and tested strategies that one can ethically employ to develop tactics of persuasion with his prospect and guide and control the conversation.

a. Gathering Intel: Every positive conversation between two humans is a result of both liking each other. This is only possible if you can gather prior intelligence about your prospect that you can put to use in your conversation to create a positive conversation. Intelligence can be (i) Preconceived (ii) Real time

In this information age, preconceived intelligence is quite easily possible thorough social media that you can use to gather information about your prospects before contacting him. Information can be about his personal interest andBusiness.

For conversations, where preconceived intelligence is not possible, one has to rely on real time intelligence and use it to his Advantage. This requires great amount of listening skills, giving your prospect a chance and space to talk.

b. Reducing Restraint: Restraint is quite obvious during conversations with strangers. It develops more in initial business Conversations, if a Sales Rep tries to sell from the beginning. This has to be addressed in the beginning of the conversation that allows the flourishing of positive communication and building of trust.

There are hundreds of different strategies to do this but the most effective one is "Likeability". If two persons are similar then they tend to develop trust for each other. Yes, similarity creates likeability which opens up gates to openness and positive rapport building whereas differences results in insecurity which is not good for sales conversations. So, every Sales Rep should make an effort to gather pre-conceived intelligence about prospects and subtly induce these in initial round of conversation to create similarity. This includes learning about prospects interests like sports or movies or politics or dressing trends etc…

This can be achieved using a combination of open and close ended targeted questions to dig deeper. A quite simpleexampleofthiswould be to ask your prospect about his business progress or about his day in the beginning of the meeting/call and then build upon the conversation to draw more information based on his responses using close and open ended questions. Then it would be a great idea to share those same challenges or interests or passion by relating it back to you and off you go.

c. Position yourself as trusted person : Last and most important piece of influencing your prospect and taking control of the conversation is to position yourself as an advisor who can be trusted by prospect for the time and energy he is going to spent listening and following you thereafter. In business, a person can trust another person in only two major situations and that is :

    i.   If you can provide a favorable gain to your prospect

    ii.   If you can save him from a greater loss.

Now, here the conversation takes a purely business route and offers a very lucrative opportunity that every Sales Rep should know how to tap on and turn it to his own advantage. At this stage, prospects would be having a good conversation experience with you and you would be at a high of the conversation and that's when you give him a bit of business talk by asking him few questions about his highest level of challenges and that is profit and loss and start throwing in numbers as to how you managed to sort a similar situation, for other similar customers to give him an idea that you can turn his situation around and you will find yourself in the driver seat.

d. Avoid Distracted Mannerism: Initial introduction with a strange person is awfully filled with strangeness and in business it also converts to nervousness and depending upon if you are dealing with an aggressive person on the other side can easily turn into inconvenience as well.

In such an environment, many salesmen have subtle habits of reacting that can be a distraction for your prospect and even worse can be seen as un-professionals like sitting postures, like shaking a leg, talking postures like biting lips etc. This should be completely avoided by practicing talking in front of a mirror or through a recording.

How to build trust with prospect

So, what is so complicated about "Prospecting & Qualification" when it comes to Sales approach? In "Prospecting & Qualification" stage, a Sales Rep requires to cross multiple hurdles to get prospect attention. As per the decision curve that a prospect needs to follow before he starts evaluating the viability of your solution or proposal, sales rep needs to cross multiple stages by providing him relevant information and help him progress over decision curve and sales funnel. The stages are highlighted below:

Get prospects attention

You can get someone attention only if you can find out what he wants to hear. But can you really do that, why not all great sales leaders have been doing this for years together. But how do they manage to do it so effectively. This is what separates then from rest of the crowd and makes them great. You can also do that by just following the below techniques that have been followed by all great leaders.

This technique is a winner and includes a 4 step process that will change your approach to prospecting and qualification for a success you never expected.

Assess

This step requires a sales rep to go through the existing accounts and list down their attributes and properties related to accounts.

For a start, you can take 50 to 100 accounts and/or also take help from your sales head and list down the attributes of each account. Attributes includes their business challenges, purchased amount, types of questions inquiredby them and stuff like that. The more attributes are there, profiling will be more precise and it will further help you understand your prospects better. This is already discussed in previous sections.

Profile

Once you have written down the attributes of all the accounts you have collected, to profile them, group them together. Grouping can be done based on Big, Small or Medium accounts or based on industry or verticals etc…This step is also crucial as the better you can profile an account, the less details you would be required to profile new accounts and provide them with the relevant details that will help you progress them down the sales funnel effectively and quickly. Refer previous sections for more details.

List Pain Points

This step involves listing down the key and top level pain points of the accounts for each of the profile you have created. It is quite important to prioritize the key pain points based on each of the profile. Once you have done that, you just need to move to the next step.

FAB mapping

FAB stands for FEATURES, ADVANTAGES and BENEFITS. FAB mapping requires you to map every pain point with the feature or list of features offered by your solution and list down the top benefits of each of the features listed down. This will allow you to talk about the benefits and advantages of each feature associated with the pain points of the profile in question.

An example of this would be, if you're a commercial real estate leasing brokerage and you're pitching to an owner, your pitch can be "Hi, I am here to discuss our plans to bring occupancy of your asset from 30% to 85% in two years." This pitch clearly demonstrates how well you have studied your prospect and crafted your concise and precise winning pitch that includes prospect highest paint points and your solution benefits.

This would be a great start for you and then you just need to ask few relevant precise questions to get the discussion extended and engage your prospect in the best possible way. Questions like

i. What have been the biggest challenges you faced with this?
ii. What drove you to look for a new provider?
iii. In what specific areas can we assist?

Get him to hear the proposal

Here you have already hooked your prospect to your solution. Now, you just have to play your cards to convert his attention into the interest. This would require you to probe more about his challenges and gather intelligence that you will use this information to profile & qualify the prospect and build upon your Sales Pitch for the current and upcoming discussions. The technique to be used here is RAMP. Yes, RAMP to successfully engaging your prospects to getting them interested in meetings and presentations.

RAMP Model

Real Time Intelligence (R)

Real Time Intelligence is the one gathered during a conversation or interaction. Here you will fire a list of questions that will help you understand your prospects current challenges by asking him more targeted open and close ended questions to assess his pain points and motivators that will drive him to buy your solution. Questions like:

i.   What challenges is your business facing and what problems do you need to solve?

ii.   What is driving your interest in our solution?

iii. How long have you had this challenge or problem? What made you decide to solve this problem now?

iv.   What objectives are you looking to achieve by solving this pain?

v.   What are the likely consequences if the requirements are not met?

It is important to note that gathering real time intelligence is not a mere act of gathering the information, it is also making an effort to engage the prospect & understand his problem statement. In

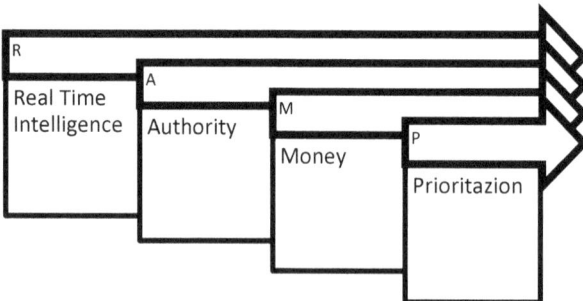

an effort to engage the prospect, you are required to address his challenges in a concise manner whenever your prospect mention about any challenge. While you are helping him with the features, it would be a smart act to throw questions along the way and gather information. This will keep your prospect hooked up while you would gather your intelligence for further steps.

Authority (A)

Authority refers to understand his company organization structure. This is important as you would like to know who the key stake holders in purchasing the solution are and stake holders in evaluating the solutions etc... Once you know who the key stake holders are, as a sales rep it would be your responsibility to reach out to them as and when you progress further in the sales funnel. Following is a good example of some of the authority related questions you can ask. Of Course, this should be customized based on your solution and process.

i.   Who else is involved in purchase decision of this solution?
ii.   How do you typically go about purchasing a solution and who is involved from accounts side?
iii.   What concerns do you think they may have? If they have any potential concerns, how do you think we should handle them?
iv.   What would be the best way to reach out to them and when?

It would be advisable to not fire all questions at the same time and confuse your prospect. Instead these should be fired at the correct timing when you consider them to be the most appropriate. Also, it would be advisable to prepare a list of questions beforehand that needs to be asked to all prospects to gather the information that is required for "Profiling" and needed to build your presentations and negotiations.

Money (M)

Once you have successfully gathered intelligence about your prospect needs, requirements and organization structure, it is time to understand their expectations of the solution based on pricing and investments. This step is crucial here because you would like to know if the organization is ready to invest in your solution otherwise, you would not like to waste your time on an opportunity that is not your cup of tea. Moreover, you would also like to assess their expectations in terms of pricing of the solution that will help you in "Deal Pricing" stage to prepare the proposal. Right set of questions can really pave the way for a fruitful discussion on this topic. Questions like:

i.   What sort of investment you are expecting on this solution?

ii.   Is there a budget already allocated for this?

iii.   Is your accounts team or CFO involved in finalizing the solution?

iv.   What is your typically purchase cycle like 2 months or more?

v.   When do you plan to ask for budget allocation for this investment?

Prioritization (P)

Prioritization is critical from the perspective that how soon prospect is planning to purchase the solution. This would be an indicator of what is the sales cycle timing you are looking at for this particular account. This will allow you to re-prioritize your other activities and accounts based on the investment potential (Money) and Sales Cycle for this account. This information will also be needed to flag the account details to the involved stake holders from your organization that might get involved in later stages.

i. Is there a contract in place already for this? If so, when is it due for renewal? And does it involve cancellation fee or any other dependencies?

ii. What is your target date for the solution implementation?

iii. Is there a target timeline you have set to close the purchase? And do you expect any delay in that due to any other priorities involved?

iv. What about the time and bandwidth for implementation?

v. Would you be interested in learning how we have helped our customers in implementation with similar requirements?

Prioritization can also be used as a tool to assess the competition and how you stack up against it. This can be done by asking the right set of questions as below:

I. Are you considering any other similar solution for this problem?

II. Do you think our solution is matching your requirements and hitting the top of the list? If not, what is lacking that you think should be fixed?

III. What are you going to do with your existing solution?

Ramp2success procedure will help you hook up your prospect and turns his attentions into his interest along with gathering intelligence that will further help you keep him engaged and convert him into paid account by preparing a killer "Deal Pricing". Here it is quite important to note that active listening skills are also of key importance along with paying key attention to every detail your prospect is sharing. Remember you have to maintain his interest in the conversation and give him space for talking.

It is also important to understand that finer details should be gathered about most critical factors like technical, economic and competitive as this will only form the foundation for making further discussions truly relevant and engaging. It is also a good habit to take a minute out after the call or meeting and make notes beforehand to avoid missing any important details. These details should also be documented clearly in your CRM for future references as you might not immediately get meeting setup with your prospect.

Meeting/Presentation commitment

By this stage, you have managed to get your prospect interested in your solution and at the same time you have profile and qualify him for the further discussions. The next step would be to convince him to setup a meet or presentation with rest of the key stakeholders involved. This can be done by offering him something that raises his interest to a level that he feels being attracted for the meeting. While there are many tactics that are being employed for this but one of them that are loved even by prospects is demonstrating how you have helped other similar customers solve the similar challenges that the prospect is facing and what additional benefits have they got from using your solution.

So, it would be suggested mentioning a name of one of your customer and asking if your prospect is aware of them. If he says yes, then it's quite simple to mention that "That's great. They are our customer and had very similar challenge when they approached us. We helped them implement our solution and now they are seeing a profit increase of X% along with productivity increase of X%"?

In fact, we can setup a meeting or presentation based on your convenience and I can showcase you how "X Customer" has used our solution and what benefits have they got. It will also help you learn about the environment that solution runs in and kind of changes you can expect. So, are you free this week or next"? You can also put across few questions on top to help your prospect decides the time and place and make him feel comfortable while getting a commitment from him.

i. So, how does your calendar look this week or next?

ii. Do you have any particular time in mind?

iii. I will send you the calendar invite along with the agenda of the meeting. Would you like me to include anyone else on the invite? And, is there anything in particular that you would like me to cover during the presentation/meeting?

iv. Do you use any internal tool for meeting setup or "my tool" will work for you?

This will ensure that you are in the driver seat of the conversation while making your prospect feel that he is being heard and understood. It will ensure that you get a commitment from the prospect about the meeting. Since, he has given the commitment; he will ensure that all stakeholders are available for the meeting.

This will also ensure that you get maximum conversions of your first call and interactions to meeting and presentations thus increasing your chances of winning accounts and that too to the maximum potential.

Presentation

Presentation stage is the next stage of the sales funnel and an important stage for any sales process. In this stage, a prospect has a Luke warm interest in your solution and practically a little idea about its value proposition, technicality and implementation. Yes, a prospect has got a taste of your solution in the first stage of "Prospecting & Qualification" and has developed familiarity with it from the introduction he has received from you. With this he understands that your solution is focused on his type of requirements which can be defined as the 'Luke warm' interest from the knowledge gained by the prospect from you.

In this stage, responsibility of a sales rep is to bring all the stake holders from both sides on one table or virtually in a conference and present his solution. This is achieved by inviting stake holders in a meeting or an online conference (much more prominent in IT industry or international selling) and demonstrating the product features and technicalities and other specific details based on type of solutions being sold.

From a prospect side, stake holders included are those involved in decision making and stake holders from vendor side included are from Marketing and Sales team, Higher Management for high priced deals, Technical and accounts heads as required.

While the task at hand is to present the solution to prospect but that is not the ultimate goal of this stage. The ultimate goal of this stage is to convert prospect's 'Luke warm' interest into a strong urge for a trial of the solution or move to the next stage of funnel (as based on your sales process).

A Sales Rep has to deal with multiple tasks in this stage like co-ordinate with multiple teams to get the presentation ready for the meeting or online webinar and then get all the stake holders join the meeting and delivering a successful presentation.

But that is just the tip of the ice Berge. There is a whole lot goes around it and a sales rep encounters multiple challenges on the way. Let's understand the major challenges presented by the stage.

Presentation Challenges
Bringing all decision makers to the Presentation

As we know that today's sales decisions are not simple anymore and involve multiple decision makers. Multiple factors like excessive competition in every domain, availability of multiple products ranging from meeting basic needs to including convenience and luxury, globalization and finally recent recessions this universe has faced, has resulted in involving multiple decision makers. And this is true for all kind of products; from as simple products as toothpaste to highly complex/priced solutions like an Air Plane. This has added fuel to the fire by making sales decision complex and difficult to handle by a sales rep.

While this looks innocent from the face of it, but has far reaching damages beyond repair like:

a. Impact on Sales Cycle

A delay faced in bringing all decision makers to the presentation or meeting can extend the Sales Cycle period. This can further result in sales rep arranging multiple distributed presentations based on decision makers interest and availability. This problem is quite significant in accounts that are not running on tight schedules. Such accounts are badly affected by this problem and such accounts can quickly see a fading response from decision makers.

b. Impact on account status

The problem of bringing all decision makers to a table is not limited to the sales cycle of an account. This can further worsen a situation for a sales rep as it results in accounts becoming inactive. This is what every sales rep hates to see an interested account becoming inactive just because of unavailability of all decision makers. An inactive account is as good as a dead account and as per a recent survey and trends, inactive accounts takes a minimum of 6 months to 2 years to revive back and regardless of the revival period, it behaves as a fresh account on revival which means the whole process starts again from the beginning and not from where it was left off.

Presenting to multiple decision makers with varied interest

While getting all decision makers to meeting/presentation is a challenge in itself but it doesn't end with having them on decision table. In fact, this marks the beginning of another episode of problem related to pitching your solution to an audience with varied interest. Yes, each decision maker is different with a varied interest:

a. Each Decision maker has different set of goals

Goals are the highest level of results that a business or a particular function of a business is aiming for. For example, a marketing function of a business can have a goal of aiming 30% market share in next 3 years and that becomes his goal. Each decision makers has its own goals based on his role and responsibility or duties he is supposed to perform in the organization which clearly define his role. Hence, his expectations of a solution and its performance driven by his responsibilities assigned. This pretty much sets his goal that he would like to achieve with the solution in question. Hence, his interest and questions will be influenced by his goals that he wishes to achieve. To give you an example,

If you are selling a CRM Solution to an organization; CRM Solution involves the following functions: Marketing, Sales and Customer Support primarily. Now, every decision maker involve will have its own set of goals like a Marketing Manager would be more interested in knowing how CRM supports his marketing goals about Lead Engagement while a Customer Support Manager would be more interested in learning about Paid customer Engagement and Customer Support history.

b. Each Decision maker has different set of challenges

Every function has different set of goals and based on their function, each one has its own set of challenges as well that they would require your solution to meet before they can agree on stress test it. Challenges are goals driven. Higher the goals are bigger the challenges it poses. In the above example of a CRM Solution, a Marketing Manager will have its own set of challenges related to Lead Engagement when aiming for 30% marketing share whereas a customer support manager might be aiming for 90% repeat business from existing customers and he would have his own set of challenges to be addressed.

c. **Each Decision makers has different set of priorities**

Priorities are driven from Challenges and they are not constant. Yes, if a business or any of its function facing a challenge of specific type, it will shift the priorities. Like challenges and priority will be different for a marketing function when launching a new product in the market than when facing a tough competition for an existing line of product. Priorities keep shifting based on the goals and challenges of a business function.

This poses a challenge for a Sales Rep to understand Goals, Challenges and Priorities of each function.

Converting prospect's Interest to Action

Last biggest challenge of a sales rep would be to engage prospects and convert their interest into action. An action can be defined as a Trial of the Product or Negotiations in case of Services or something else based on specific sales processes in B2B and B2C space. It is a challenge in itself to incorporate individual interest into a presentation or meeting but the much bigger challenge is how to convert that interest into an action. A Sales Rep needs to find an answer to the core questions like:

1. Whatare the drivers that can engage a prospect?and
2. What are the drivers that push him for an action?

These challenges have to be addressed before you can expect your prospect to respond to your call for action for the next step. So, what is the solution to these challenges? How can a Sales rep get around these challenges and win over his prospect?

"Authority" is the answer that motivates a prospect to fall in love with your product such that he cannot ignore to try it or buy it.

Authority

The doctor bent over the lifeless figure in bed. Then he straightened up and said, "I am sorry to say that your husband is no more, my dear."

A feeble sound of protest came from the lifeless figure in bed: "No, I'm still alive. "Hold your tongue." said the woman. "The doctor knows better than you."

That is the power of "Authority".

Ever wondered:

- Why prospects leave a vendor before even trying out their product?
- Why most companies struggle to get prospect time to try out their product and still fail to do so even though they have the best product in the market?
- Why prospects turn back from the table even before they give a serious attention to the product?

A Prospect needs a better solution for his or her company requirements. Finding out a solution and betting his time and money on it before he can find out how it is going to perform in his own environment needs a strong confidence and that confidence comes from Brand Authority.

However, not every brand is a Microsoft or Apple. Then how does a prospect get a feel of the brand authority? It is the Sales Rep who owns this responsibility on behalf of his company.

A Sales Rep is considered as a Brand Ambassador who carries the responsibility of introducing his company's brand authority in terms of company products, company culture and company's competitiveness to the prospect. If a Sales Rep is failing to give this confidence, you would see more and more prospects turning back from the table regardless of how effective your marketing funnel is or how efficient your website or products are.

Being a brand ambassador is about establishing your brand authority at every step of the sales funnel that keeps the prospect glued to the brand and keep pushing him for more – and that's a Sales Rep ultimate goal. But how does a Sales Rep can establish his Authority over a prospect such that he can be pushed down the funnel to try and buy the product. In the coming section, we will study how a Sales Rep can establish his authority and make use of it to drive conversions.

What makes a person Authoritative?

If knowledge is POWER, then a GOD AM **I** - Jim Carry [Batman Forever]

There are several factors that works together to make a person authoritative. Some works independently and can be used to assert authority whereas other works concurrently. To understand what are those factors and how one can use them to assert its authority over others to convince prospects; we need to first understand different type of authorities that humans readily accept without questioning it. It is important to understand that the authority should be unquestionable otherwise it is not authority at all.

So, let's take a look at the various authorities that exists in personal and business space and drive us to trust and follow others.

Types of Authority

There are prominently two different types of authorities that we typicallycome acrossand establishour trust in a person. These authorities then influence our decisions when we deal with them.

Command

If you have been stopped by a policeman on the way to your home and being asked to report to the police station immediately; do you think you will question it or worst deny it. The best chances are you won't. Why? It is the authority that comes with the uniform that enables one person to stop or question any other person and we have to accept it. This type of authority is referred as "Command" authority.

Command authority is the one which comes with the formal position a person is holding like a CEO of the company. It is implied that orders from formal positions will be followed without any denial.

Expert

This is the type of authority which comes from having vast knowledge on a particular topic or industry etc. This authority implies that you know about something better than others and hence it is implied that you are an expert and should be followed. This type of authority that can be built by any person unlike "Command" authority and mostly used to gain trust of other people and ultimately followers who believes in what you believe and follows you unquestionably.

Have you ever questioned a doctor about the medicines prescribed by him for any of your illness you have faced? I bet never. Nobody does it. We just trust him and follow him for he is the expert of the field and has an unquestionable authority in our eyes that make us trust and follow him.

This is the authority that is possessed by Top Sales Leaders; TopSales Influencers like Grant Cardone, Dave Stein, Brian Tracy, Tom Hopkins, and Victor Antonio to name a few that not just makes them great but forces the industry to trust them and follows them without a doubt. You can get it too. You just need to know how to work towards it and once you get a hang of it, you will be invincible. You will turn yourself into a magnet that attracts prospects, a conversion engine that just converts any account he puts his hand on. So, stay tuned as we discuss on how to establish your authority in the next section.

Establish your Authority

Establishing authority is an altogether different ball game. It is difficult but then this is the only way you can win prospect confidence to surrender him to you. In this process of establishing your authority over prospect and confide him in you, a sales rep require an unconquerable demonstration of knowledge and information to the prospect that proves to be vital for a prospect to realize the tangible and intangible values and benefits he will receive by associating himself with your brand. Once he realizes that, you would not be required to run after prospect, chasing him for an action; nor gets worried thinking about competition approaching him. None of that will matter and your supremacy will continue to rule your prospect mind before and after the purchase of your solution.

You must remember that a prospect looks for a confidence in the brand and once he gets it, he will be ready to overlook minor limitations associated with your product. However, this requires a sales Rep to produce high quality information for his prospect that is of tangible value like actionable intelligence and it is equally important that it should be accurate.

Also, we should never forget that a Sales Rep responsibility is to maintain integrity when delivering any information to the prospect. Always remember that a prospect is always moved by your confidence and authority but it doesn't mean that he doesn't already know that information or will not cross verify it. If you believe in this trick, you and your brand will be the "ULTIMATE" looser and you might end up paying a very heavy price for this stupid mistake. Trust me – I have seen many cases of this ultimate stupidity where a Sales Rep mistaken a prospect to be unaware and tries to fool around by passing information that is not true or doesn't exist and end up paying heave price for this foolishness.

So, let us study the type of information that is easily available to a sales rep and how to use it to establish him/her as an authority in front of a prospect that will allow him/her to win accounts consistently like a Pro.

A Business faces multiple challenges at each level or has aspiring goals at each level that it is looking to fulfill through a solution which is offered by you. These goals or challenges are the motivators for a decision maker to dedicate his or her energy, time and money to a solution or another business vendor.

From the previous discussion on Presentation stage challenges, we understand that a presentation or meeting about a solution needs to address the requirements of multiple decision makers with varied interest driven by goals or challenges they face. The most effective way of achieving this such that not only your presentation is relevant to their requirements but also appealing, is to understand business goals and challenges types at each level of a business and how to incorporate these to be addressed in your presentation/meeting.

Business decision about a solution purchase involves decision makers from mid and senior level management. Functions involved are purely driven by the type of solution offered. However, all business goals or challenges can be categorized in the following categories to be included in your presentation and make it relevant and appealing to all type of audience.

Business Challenges

Strategic

Strategic Goals or Plans are the top level plans that are designed keeping in mind the entire organization. These goals are in existence to meet the long term vision of an organization. These goals are set at the top level by the top level executives of the organization like CEO or President of the organization. These goals work as a framework for the entire organization to build their strategies around it that are aligned with the overall goals of the organization and can make the organization more effective.

Organizational level strategic goals can include but not specific to:

    i.   Achieving Growth
    j.   Improving Productivity
    k.   Increasing Profitability
    l.   Increasing Return on Investment

Hence, when pitching to a high level company executive like CEO or President, it is quite important that your presentation should represent how your solution advantages and benefits are aligned to increase organization growth/profitability or productivity or Return on Investment of an Organization. Any top level executive would be interested in meeting his top level goals and if the benefits are clearly aligned to the top level goals or challenges of an organization then they would find it very appealing such as it will be an actionable insight for them to move forward and expedite the decision making process and that is the goal of a presentation stage.

To understand how this can be achieved, imagine you are selling a backup Solution (a software solution to help organization backup and secure their data and information assets) to a mid-size organization and pitching the solution to a decision maker who is a C-Level executive. To a C-Level executive Business Up time (Business Performance) is more important than the investment. So, your sales pitch in presentation should be focused on highlighting:

Business Uptime: Your solution can help them maintain a business uptime of 99.9% annually by offering the following features. Now, business performance is of utmost importance to any C-Level executive and your pitch will make sure he is connected.

This would clearly communicate the kind of benefit that you bring to the table and your target audience will find it very appealing.

Tactical

Now that we understand the Strategic Goals and Challenges an organization can face and how to pitch to the top level executives. Let's look into the Tactical level goals and challenges that mid-level manager looks to address that can be used by a Sales Rep to design presentation that is both relevant and appealing to the mid-level managers.

Tactical Goals or Plans are the one level down to the Strategic goals and sits between Strategic and Operational goals. These goals act as support to the Strategic goals for an organization and designed at mid-level by translating Strategic Plans into actionable activities.

Let us take the same example as above to understand what Tactical goals within an organization are; in the above example consider an organization is aiming for business uptime. Its IT Manager understands the high level goals of an organization. However, as an IT manager his own goals are to reduce the Annual IT budget to half but maintain or increase the business performance. So, he looks for annual spending of IT budget on all tools. Here a Sales Rep pitch can be focused on how the IT budget can get reduced by implementing your solution while the business performance increases or stays the same without any impact.

Hence, it is ensuring that a C-Level executive as well as mid-level manager hooked up to your presentation and feeling your authority at the same time.

Operational

Operational goals sit at the bottom of the hierarchy and are prepared and maintained by the lower level managers and executives. These goals can be as short as daily, monthly or quarterly goals. Daily operational task such as maintaining employees attendance, performance, maintain inventory, building monthly budget, developing and maintaining promotional activities are few of the examples.

Assuming you are in conversation or presenting the solution to all decision makers that includes lower level managers then you can highlight features that automate daily or weekly task like in backup solution example above, you can highlight that daily scheduling of backup job is one time effort and not necessarily done every day. This will be of interest to them.

Financial

At the end of the day, everything boils down to money. Financial goals are part of each and every function and all level of managers. Budgeting and Profitability is everybody's responsibility in an organization and hence your presentation should focus delicately on this aspect. However, just talking about the price alone will not make your presentation appealing. There is a lot more to it that you need to include and that requires a bit of work from your side.

All levels of managers hold the responsibility of budgeting which is allocating and spending the budget wisely. Hence, at the end of everything, everybody would be interested in knowing how solution is priced but like I said just mentioning the price to them doesn't make you an authority and gets them interested in your solution. What will really have them moving would be if you can show them that you truly understand all aspect related to money and what impact it will have on their budgets if they buy your solution. And if you can show this to them, prospects would be very interested in your solution. These aspects are:

1. TCO

TCO stands for Total Cost of Ownership. TCO is a financial estimate intended to help buyers and owners determine the direct and indirect costs of a product or system. This is an indicator to a buyer as to how much they need to spend on your solution including all type of costs. If you can mention about this in your presentation or meeting then this indicator will help them understand the cost involved. This information can be gathered from the existing customer accounts and with the help of your managers.

2. Break Even

Breakeven analysis is used to determine when a business will be able to cover all its expenses and begin to make a profit in a particular investment. It is an indicator of a period after which all the costs involved in the solution will be recovered.

3. ROI

Return on investment, or ROI, is the most common profitability ratio. This shows how much money you will have after withdrawing your investment, again in consideration of fees taxes, etc. ROI can be negative, zero or positive. There are several ways to determine ROI, but the most frequently used method is to divide net profit by total assets. So if your net profit is $100,000 and your total assets are $300,000, your ROI would be .33 or 33 percent.

Role of Case Study and Testimonials

Till now we have 'talked the talk' but now we will 'walk the talk'. Every prospect has this question in mind and would love to hear your success stories that would be like a mark on the stone for him. So, it would be great idea to share your existing customer's case studies and testimonials. We should remember that Case Studies are the key here and Sales Rep reliance should not be on testimonials. Testimonials are just comments of happy customers giving an idea about your great product and/or service but this is no replacement to case study. Case study actually is relevant here and demonstrates how your solution has made an impact to a business that has helped them gain a momentum. This would further excite the prospect.

So, what should be highlighted as part of the case study that is exciting to the prospect? It is quite simple and step by step information is highlighted that makes a great case study and compliment your presentation.

    i.   Select a customer that is a close match to the prospect in question and if possible familiar to the prospect.

    j.   Pick and highlight two or three strategic/Tactical/Operational level business challenges that are again a close match that customer faced before he contacted you.

k. If possible highlight his existing solution provider used by customer and any additional support or service related issues faced by customer.

l. Highlight the key metrics before your solution is implemented by the customer.

m. Highlight how your solution helped them solve their major challenges

n. Highlight what were the results of the key metrics after the solution is implemented.

o. Highlight additional financial gains customer received by partnering with you.

p. Highlight the customer testimonial about your solution and service.

If your preparation, presentation/meeting is just focused around these aspects then you are in the game to win. This will make you an authority in front of your prospect as you clearly, deeply understand each aspect of their business and challenges and your solution will be a great attraction to them as it is completely focused on their interest. The result will be, prospects will completely confide in you and will be connected to move further.

Create 'Value Proposition'

A value proposition is a promise of value to be delivered and acknowledged by vendor and a belief from the prospect that value will be delivered and experienced.

The doze of addressing prospects business challenges through your solution benefits is good enough for prospects to realize your command over your field and the potential of your solution for their needs. This will straight away put you in control over your prospects thinking. And at this stage, demonstrating your solution value proposition would prove to be icing on the cake for your prospect.

Value Proposition is a combination of:

i.   Relevancy: This factor explains how your product solves prospect's problems or improves their situation.
j.   Quantified Value: This factor determines how your solution delivers specific benefits.
k.   Unique differentiation: It tells the ideal prospect why theyshouldbuy from you and not from the competition

In the previous sections we have seen how a Sales Rep can address the 'Relevancy' and 'Quantified Value' delivered by the solution. In this section, we will discuss unique differentiation or the unique value delivered by the solutionthat position you above your competition.

Competition is part of the game and vendor as well as prospect is aware of it. Competition has become enormous due to globalization and it is right next to you due to advancements in technology (primarily INTERNET). A Prospect, regardless of the size of deal or requirement he has, typically engages with 2 to 3 vendors at least during the course of RFP (Request for Proposal).

Hence, it is quite obvious that a prospect would like to understand how you are placed better than the competition or precisely what value you deliver that is unique to you. So, let's take a look at what factors a Sales Rep should include in his presentation to stand out and win prospect confidence in him and his solution.

A comparison with the competitor is interesting. You have the comparison details as well but the big question remains "how a prospect would like to hear it?" Well that's not too complicated either. In my experience of dealing with hundreds and thousands of prospects, one thing is clear that everybody is interested in hearing only two things:

i.   Current benefits

ii.   Future Gains

So, a sales rep has to encapsulate everything that is worth comparing within the current unique benefits and future gains of the partnership for the prospect. This should be the "Holy Grail", your framework to demonstrate what unique your partnership has to offer that stands out in the market. This should pretty much get you started.

The next step would be what is worth comparing with your competitor that raises your prospect eyebrow. Well, there are general things that fit every type of sales process regardless of the industry and solution being sold and then there are specific things to the solution, industry in question. We will stick to the general things that fit any type of sale process and will serve as a great platform upon which you should be able to build industry or solution specific benefits.

a. Features and Benefits comparison

Features and benefits comparison sets the tone by forming the bases and gives your prospect an idea of the major features and benefits comparison. It is important to highlight only the key benefits and keep it precise and not to flood it with the information.

b. Pricing and financial gain comparison

This is a crucial comparison as prospect would be   interested to know investments comparison and current and future financial gains he can expect using your solution.

c. Support and Maintenance comparison

With an ever closing competition, Support and Maintenance have become the "X Factor" of the Value Proposition. A Prospect would be keen to know the level and type of support and maintenance offered to him, at what price and what differentiate you from your competition.

d. Brand Reputation comparison

This is more of an informal comparison in terms of pre presentation. While it iskeyto highlight thisduringyour presentation but should not be elaborated more than required. Key factors should be highlighted like how your brand is perceived as compared to your competitor. To give you an example, Audi is perceived as luxury whereas Maruti is value for money.

e. Shakeups comparison

Shakeups are things that have gone wrong for your competition and will be of very specific interest to your prospect. And, believe me, this can be a big differentiator. Shakeups include a failed release for the particular solution in question, complaints on support, quality complaints or company culture complaints.

This information can be gathered from competitor's website in specific areas like Blogs, Forums etc... This type of information will also be available in other public forums and Social Media pages and groups that you can access easily.

f. Industry/Segment focus comparison

Industry focus comparison at times can really   prove beneficial if there is a difference between industry focus as compared to your competition. This information is also crucial for your prospect and he might not be even aware of it simply by browsing website. A prospect completely relies on sales rep for this.

An example of this would be Apple and Microsoft. Apple product focuses on high end market and that's why their products are expensive. At the same time, their focus is more on consumer market than business whereas Microsoft is focused on low and mid-size consumer and business markets.

g.   Future Plans comparisons

Every business has its own focus and directions. It changes with business and market performance. Your competitor might have same market focus as yours today but his business performance or goals might have him change it tomorrow. This creates a good opportunity to score above your competition in your conversations and presentations. But it is hard to find out and you need to constantly study your competitor moves through their announcements on their website and social media pages.

h.   Financial Stability comparison

A business partnership is like a marriage and any prospect would be wary of a business financial stability if the brand is not popular enough to eliminate this doubt. While this may not be enquired directly by the prospect, however this information can give a Sales Rep an edge over competition if he can find this information out which is usually very difficult.

This information should help you position well in front of your prospect. It is quite important to know that a Sales Rep requires to have multiple resources to have access to above information that includes competitor website, social media pages, forums, public forums etc… but one source which is not yet highlighted is "Your Existing Customers" who have used your competitor products in the past before coming to you are a great, perennial and most accurate and reliable source of information for you.

During my decade long experience, I have seen most of the organizations have ignored this or have not fully tapped into the potential of information that your existing customer possesses. This is primarily due to the fact that the information received by vendors are not organized and turned into actionable insight. If the information from the customer can be turned into actionable insight, it can help Sales Team excel in selling plus helps organizations better understand their competitive space for outperforming competition. As a Sales Rep it is quite important for you to maintain touch with existing customers and keep pulling information that can help you sell better. Information can be organized in the above format to be used effectively.

This comparison put together forms a great asset for a Sales Rep as well as prospect to clearly understand how the two brands compare to each other and give a complete idea why he should be going with you. This also makes him believe that knowledge that you as a Sales Rep possesses and how you are playing a role of a trusted advisor whom he can rely on for any information to make him an effective decision.

Be a great Presenter

A great story is a successful ingredient but we have seen great stories falling apart when not presented properly. We have seen the information above that is great enough to hook up your audience to you regardless of the platform – online, offline or public speaking etc… However, there are other rules of the games that you need to learn to be a great presenter. This will ensure that your audience is hooked up all the time and you have their complete attention and drive them crazy by just following the simple techniques highlighted below.

1. Content is the key: Color is the life. White plain text presentations are boring and a true killer. Colorful presentation with pictures and if possible videos truly attract your audience. Also, visual memories last long. So, make use of it and make your presentation colorful with images and videos.

2. Presentation should be engaging: Just listening is boring. Your audience will fall asleep if you are the only one who is speaking regardless of how much ever great speaker you are. Spice up your presentation with quick surveys, Q&A etc… to make it truly engaging.

3. Reward attendees for attending the presentation and taking part in presentation. This should not be a big gift but small discounts, limited access to paid information or such small things will be a good gesture for thanking them for their time. It is a good practice to announce this in the beginning of the presentation. Works beautifully in online presentations especially.

4. Introduce the Next Step: End of the Presentation is not the end of it. It is the beginning of the next step for the prospect and next phase for you. So, include it in your presentation and educate your prospects a little about

it. This will ensure they are ready for it before you ask
it.

5. Delivering time bound presentation: Time is money for
    your prospects and he doesn't have all day to spend
    with you. So, respect that fact and set expectation of
    the schedule and time of presentation and try to finish
    it in time.

6. Body Language: Body gesture speaks louder than you
    and it forms a key aspect of your presentation
    regardless of the platform. A feeble voice is seen
    conscious and nervous. A closed body gesture like arms
    tied to your chest and foot stick to each other are seen
    as a gesture of nervousness and works against you.
    Relaxed and open body gestures with loud and emotion
    filled voice is a mark of confidence.

7. Ensure your equipment like laptops, ppt in case of face
    to face presentation and headsets, online tools and
    network in case of online meetings should be in order
    before you get started. This can prove fatal if any of it
    fails during the presentation.

It is advisable to practice your presentation at least two times
before you go ahead with it. A mock test in the few initial
meetings with an expert like your manager can really help you gain
the momentum and grip to master the art of presentation.

Trial

Customer Onboarding has come up a long way. There has been a complete power shift from vendors to prospects due to emerging markets, technologies and competitions. This power shift has resulted in 'try before you buy' for almost all kind of solutions being sold by business except few consumers and business products that is impossible to try before you buy like a soap or a big centralized AC kind of stuff.

"Try before you buy" has gone so deep into the "Customer Engagement" process that you cannot imagine a sale or an account win without it. However, we have seen brands still not able to tap its full potential and prospect churn is high and increasing for all types of high and low touch brands. Sure, they did try to control the churn by implementing automation software and sharing product features, technical information related articles and how to guides to keep prospects engaged but what is the result. The result is zero to minimal effect.

We are dealing with humans and not machines; humans that are professionals, have priorities, needs hand holding and believes in user experience. Hence sharing few articles will not get you the best outcome that you wish for. Here, a Sales Rep holds the responsibility to motivate prospects to try his solution as once a prospect tries a solution, it increases your chances of getting a sales multiple times unless it is an inferior solution, an irrelevant solution or you failed to deliver an experience that motivate him to buy like bad to no customer service. So, how can a Sales Rep ensure that prospects try your solution and buy it?

Thegolden key to open this lock is 3C – Commit – Coordinate – Control. Let us see how a sales rep can use these to unlock the success to engage and win accounts during trial of the product.

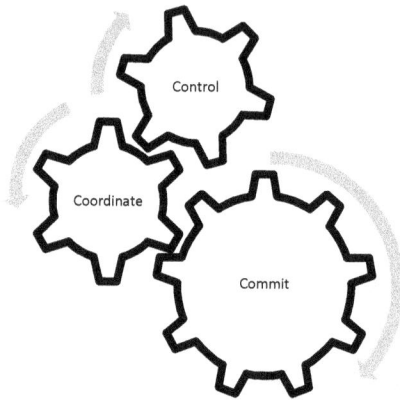

Commit

Commitment is big thing for anyone. In business, it is even bigger and creating a sense of commitment drives prospects and sales reps to do things for each other as it is considered a sense of responsibility and not meeting the commitment creates a bad impression. A Sale Rep can use this as a tool to engage prospect in a trial commitment to try a link and sell the entire chain.

After a successful meeting or presentation, it is not hard enough to get your prospect to commit for the trial and that should be your first focus. Let's see in what situations, a prospect feels your trial proposal a commitment that would get him to meet it.

First Step to Trial

Have you ever wondered when we meet a stranger directly or through someone we know, we undergo an informal commitment that we won't ignore him next time we meet him. Yes, that is an informal commitment. This works in business as well and does wonders as to how human psychology is driven by this informal commitment. So, how can you make use of it?

The best way to make this informal commitment work for you is to ask your prospect the following questions right after the meeting/presentation when he is best connected to you and supercharged after your great presentation.

> a. When do you wish to start the trial of the solution?

> b. Who will be heading the trial? Is he with us in the meeting or someone else?

If he is someone already present in the meeting then that is the best thing that can happen. If not then you should find out who is he?

> c. Can you share his details with me so I can connect with him offline to take this further?

> d. Can you do me a favor of sending short mail introducing me to him so he is not surprised when he hears from me?

And this will ensure multiple benefits for you as a Sales Rep that will do wonders for you.

> a. Your prospect has automatically gone into an informal commitment with you to carry this forward which is in 95% cases he will oblige to it.

> b. The person who would be heading the trial has also gone into an informal commitment with you to take up the trial immediately and seriously as the instructions are coming directly from his boss.

This will ensure that you are on right path to engage your prospect in the trial of the solution in the most perfect way. Additionally, you now know whom to interact with to take it forward and he is also aware of you. So, now you just need to make a contact and take this forward.

Coordinate

Coordinating a trial is the list of activity that is performed to help the designated person perform a successful trial in an effective way such that it increases your chances of winning the deal and at the same time, it should shorten the decision cycle. However, most business and sales rep leave it to the fate which leads to churn and they don't even realize it.

As per one of the survey, in 95% cases, a solution trial for the designated person is an additional responsibility over and above his daily task to be performed. This is especially 100% true in small and mid-size deals. This task when seen as an additional responsibility by the designated person, he might try to get rid of it quickly or try to postpone it based on the priorities or even worse try to ignore it resulting in an extended sales cycle or a deal killer.

To avoid this, a Sales Rep has to be on his toes to connect with the designated person on time, help him see this task as a breeze by helping him with all the details and makes the experience memorable that a positive report is sent to decision makers by him. This requires a Sales Rep to follow the below loop to make it a successful trial.

Trial Plan

A Sales Rep should connect with the designated person when the timing is right, soon after you have been introduced to him and he is updated on the trial. Create a conversation to understand his trial plan and how he defines the success in trial. Success in trial is testing of limited product features, in few typical case scenarios which hold priority for the business. This Intel is critical and will dictate the rest of the trial and support framework offered during the trial.

Setting up trial experience

The next logical step is to assist your prospect (designated person for the trial) with the details of the trial. This will includes setting up the trial, running the trial, testing the use cases. A Sales Rep should assist him with all the documentations and thought leadership available to make the trial easy and successful.

However, before the prospect get started with the trial using the docs provided, he should be provided with a short demo on how to implement the solution and use features with the use cases he is planning. This will ensure he is not wasting time shooting in dark. This will also ensure a much better experience for him which he will love as you are helping him perform his duties in the best possible way.

Offer Great Support

A Sales rep next task would be to ensure that his prospect is receiving great support throughout the trial. This is ensured by introducing support point of contact for all kind of his queries to him. This will make him feel free about approaching correct person to get faster response than writing to a general mail box and waiting for people to understand his requirements and respond.

The best timing to introduce your support contacts to the prospect would be during the demo presentation you have arranged for him.

Control

You have ensured that your prospect is getting all the help that is needed but is that enough. You are dealing with an opportunity which is hot and soon going to convert into a sale. Would it be wise to not to exercise any control over it. What would happen if you do not control it? There are many possibilities I have seen across all types of businesses and situations happening when Sales Rep do not exercise any control or slow to react assuming that trial is running smooth and prospect doesn't need any help.

1. Prospect run into an issue and forgot to get in touch with you – this will prolong your sales cycle.

2. Something else has taken priority at prospect end and the project is been put on to the back burner without being assigned to someone else– again a delay in sales cycle or worse is no sale.

3. Prospect runs into an issue, contacts your team but a glitch blocked the communication and nobody is aware of it. This can be a technology glitch or human error.

The end result will be delay in sale or no sale at all – hitting your monthly quota badly. This is one of the major cause for approximately 20% churn (that's huge) during the trial and the irony is that it is the most simple to handle and avoid just by exercising a little control. Let's see how you can do it.

Trail Signup

Trail Signup is done by prospect to test drive the product or solution. Based on the type of solution, trial can be downloaded from the website, or Sales Rep demonstrate the product. However, one thing to be noted and important is – Trail signup should be simple involving very few steps to setup and should be no brainer. Otherwise, this might degrade your prospect interest and activeness to start the trial and your efforts to present your solution and engaging the prospect can go in vain.

Maintain prospect interest

Prospect interest is to evaluate the solution to the pre-defined use cases based on business priorities and issue a report with recommendations. For this he needs your assistance to help setup and run the trial. Based on the current trends, business share preset information with the prospects regardless of their requirements and needs. This is done through the marketing automation software that has preset templates that is automatically shared through email or other means with the prospect which might add value to prospect trial but this is not always true in most of cases.

A Sales Rep is closer to the prospect and has a complete understanding of his needs, challenges and use cases they are looking to try out. This information can be used to share articles that help your prospect to perform his trial successfully, relate to his use cases and help him reduce the trial period will be much appreciated. And if it is coming from his most trusted source, he will be delighted.

This will not only maintain his interest and prove to be of help to him but also motivates him to try those features in trial and produce a successful report and gain his employer appreciation – everyone wants that type of motivation and if you can offer this opportunity to him then he will be glad to rewards you for the efforts through positive report and appreciating your efforts.

Looping Decision Maker

Do you only keep your engagement limited to the designated person till the trial is finished and then contact the actual decision maker? I have seen most of the Sales Reps doing this. But what is the harm in this?

After the trial is over, did you ever encountered situations like repeating the whole process of presentation just because the prospect lost the track and needs a memory refresh before he can proceed with decision making? Even worse new decision makers will enter the scene this time only to delay the decisions further and the story goes on…

In many cases I have seen that for projects that are not a priority for a business are not dedicatedly handled by the designated person and decision makers might also not be aware of it. This proves fatal and delays the decision making.

This can be completely avoided in almost all the situations by constantly reporting progress from your side to the decision maker. This keeps him on track with the progress and he will be committed to keep this project on the top of his agenda. This will avoid any delays in decision making as he would be checking back the progress internally and you know that how seriously it will be dealt internally when the boss himself is on top of it.

It will also position you and your organization as highly regarded professionals in prospects eyes and will have current and future benefits once he becomes your customer. This will also help you stand out from the competition just because you are so committed to your job.

Negotiations and Closing

Negotiations

This is a show of wishes and emotions. In fact, negotiations are like a tug of war of wishes and emotions between you and your prospect. The only question stands is who is the winner?

A negotiation is a phase where a Sales Rep is required to understand prospects requirements and his potential thoroughly; provide him with the offer that truly holds value for your prospect and he readily agree for it or in other words creates a win-win situation for both prospect and vendor. The key here is the offer that holds value for your prospect and is viable/profitable for your company otherwise you will end up getting a least possible investment from your prospect or even worst losing the deal. Negotiations aren't easy. It is easy if you are ready to agree to all demands of your prospect and get him onboard but it is difficult if you would like to get your prospect onboard on your terms.

A recent survey on sales conversion has this to say "only 8% of sales rep converts 80% of sales". This has been so true from the time immemorial. This is possible because the 8% Sales Rep either are born negotiators or they completely understood and mastered the complex yet entertaining art of negotiations and how to tap the potential of it fully to gain accounts without being at loss. How do they do it?

Children are considered to be the best negotiator. Ever wondered how they manage to convince you or anyone to get what they want. How easily they can blackmail you for chocolates either by crying out in public or showering heaven full of love on you. What is that makes you bend so easily for any demand they have and without a choice to move out, you surrender yourself to their demands.

It's possible because they have a wish for which they are ready to go to any extent and unknowingly play with your emotions. Yes, it is a show of wishes and emotions and whoever understands it better comes out as a winner. So, let us understand the logical flow of emotions across the negotiations process and how one can understand, control and master it to convert more and convert better.

Initiate 'Proposal Discussion'

Do you wait for the prospect to come back to you or drop you an email uttering those golden words "We are ready to move forward with it; what's next?" If that is how you have been handling your pipeline then know this that there is an opportunity for you to bring down your sales cycle by 25% to 35%.

Once you have your prospect get going with the trial, a Sales Rep is tasked with two things to run parallel:

> a. Support your prospect during the trial

> b. Find an opportunity to bring your prospect to negotiation table as early as possible.

In this age of trials and test drives, every company has a 'Test Run' to offer to their prospect which typically lasts from 2 weeks to 1 month or more depending upon the product. However, Sales Rep goal is not to wait for prospect to come back after the trial and gift you the order. If a prospect has to come back confirming his acceptance to move to negotiations then that can take Trail +

2weeks or even longer as it depends upon many situations. You do not want that to happen.

Your actual aim is to bring the prospect to negotiation table before the trial ends and not after it. And, to bring your prospect to the negotiation table requires you to look for signals that confirm your prospect is mentally ready for the proposal to move into to negotiation phase though he might not reveal it. So, how do you find out if your prospect is ready or not?

1.   Every prospect well plan their evaluation phase. Plan of evaluation will base on their current business requirements and complexity of the product in question. Hence, based on requirements, each prospect has a list of requirements or can be called as list of features that they look for in their product and wish to test it to ensure its feasibility for their requirements.

These features can be divided into:

a.   Critical requirements – High Priority
b.   Must have features – Medium Priority
c.   Good to have features – Least Priority

Evaluation of your solution is completely driven by these requirements. And, this is where a Sales Rep is required to pitch in and bring him to the negotiation table. Hence, during initial round of discussions with the decision makers, a Sales Rep is required to prepare this list of requirements that fits the above categories. This list should also be validated with the person designated for the trial to ensure if you are spot on or any changes are required. While keeping the track of the trail and supporting your prospect along the way, a Sales Rep just needs to ensure that critical requirements have been tested and tested first. And, from this stage a Sales Rep can start pitching in for the negotiations.

This type of information is an actionable intelligence for a Sales Rep to bring their prospect on negotiations at the right time. Of course, there would be few exceptions to this as few of your prospects would like to complete the test but majority of your accounts will ripe quicker and will agree to be on negotiation table approvingly.

Features list preparation done in the initial discussions, will also help you to support your prospect trial in the best possible way by guiding them through evaluating the features and sharing knowledge articles that supports and compliments their trial.

2. We have seen how being in touch with the decision maker helps a Sales Rep exercise control over the deal. A Prospect reaction to the trial progress updates shared by you also accounts for the signals for initiating the negotiation stage. A prospect demonstrating satisfaction over trial progress and mentioning it to you provides you an opportunity to pull him into negotiations by asking "Well now that trial progress is satisfactory, would you like me to start working on your quotation and send it across to you by end of this week".

Design Proposal Strategy

So, you have understood positive signals and managed to pull your prospect onto negotiation table well before the trial is over and now he is ready to receive proposal from you. Is that all? That's only the half battle won. The struggle actually starts from here. This is the stage where every Sales Rep wishes for maximum investment from the prospect. Whereas on the prospect side, he is faced with two challenges, how much to invest in the solution and how he can get the most in the least possible investment avoiding any risk. So, the actual battle of wishes and emotions starts from here. Why I have been calling it a battle because it is indeed a battle for a Sales Rep as well as the prospect to protect his investment as much as possible without losing any value. So, a Sales Rep is encountered with two difficult choices and that is:

Split the Pie

This is traditional way of handling sales negotiations and we have known this for a very long time. In this negotiation technique, there is a tug-of-war between the prospect and the sales rep to decide who gets the bigger share. A prospect is fighting for the maximum value in the least investment possible whereas a Sales Rep is fighting for the maximum investment possible.

Expand the Pie

This is what I have been teaching all the way and have seen all the best sales leaders following the same and differentiating them from the rest to get more and get better from the prospect. Top Sales leaders have mastered this art of expanding the pie that truly creates a Win-Win situation for both the prospect and the Sales Rep. So, what is exactly expanding the Pie.

In this technique, a Sales Rep creates multiple offers that are above the prospect expectations and potential but truly offering an increasing value that is difficult to resist for the prospect. Prospect wins by getting more value and a Sales Rep wins by getting more investment and more than that prospect's trust and happiness that will continue to reward the vendor in all future purchases. This is how a true Sales Leader gets more and better conversions.

However, the key to be a winner using the "Expand the Pier" technique lies in 3 things.

    a.   Information - Correctly predicting a prospect potential and expectations

This is the most crucial part of negotiations. A Sales Rep need to prepare a proposal and to prepare a proposal he needs to have a complete understanding of prospect's potential. Without any idea of prospect's potential, a Sales Rep can never get a proposal right and this only leads to confusion and later on forcing prospect to lose his confidence and restrict him to invest to minimum. You do not wish for that.

In sales world, a prospect potential in colloquial terms refer to the estimate of his current requirements. A Sales Rep gather this information during initial discussions and keep updating it during the entire engagement. So, what is considered to be the information that represents true potential?

There are multiple types of actionable intelligence that a Sales Rep can gather from the prospect directly or indirectly to estimate prospect potential. To start with,

    i.   Prospect current operation size and setup.

This is a great indicator of prospect's current requirements. However, it requires a Sales Rep to estimate prospects current investment size based on the size of the operation. This is not hard do it and trying it for one or two time should get you into practice of estimating is correctly. Existing Customers data of similar size, industry and operation can be a good start to get the estimates right.

    ii. Prospects investment size in his existing solution.

This is very straight forward and a good indicator of current investments. A Sales Rep is required to capture this information in the initial discussions to be used to precisely estimate the potential.

    iii. Budget allocated for solution investment and total budget for the department.

This is also an important indicator of prospect's current requirements. A Sales Rep is required to gather information related to current budget allocation for solution investment and/or budget allocated for the entire function. This can be used to prepare estimates and proposals for the prospect.

This should put you on path to correctly estimate the current requirements of the prospect and prepare the proposal for it. While this information is helpful for current requirement estimation, it is not at all sufficient for creating a winning proposal for the prospect. To create winning proposals for the prospect, you would require knowing additionally the following information:

Assess Future Requirements

To be a sales leader, a Sales Rep should be in the practice of winning accounts above the current potential. This is possible if a Sales Rep can estimate the future or rather near future requirements expansion of the prospect and pitch him the proposal with value. If this happens, then there is no way a prospect would reject the proposal. But how do you do it?

The best way to estimate the future requirements would be to gather comparative analysis on the above information. This is explained below.

1. Operation Size and Setup
2. Existing competitor solution investment
3. Budget Allocation

A Sales Rep is required to capture information about above parameters for the current year and how it has grown in the last two years. This will be helpful for you to predict the growth for the next 1 year and 3 years and prepare a proposal for the prospect.

An example would be, a Business A has done a recent investment of $500,000 in their existing solution. The investment has been growing 20% YoY (Year on Year). So, your proposal for 1 year would be $600,000 (including 20% growth) and for 3 years would be $800,000.

Additionally, a Sales Rep should also gather information on budget estimates for the coming year or next year. This information will also be helpful in putting together a proposal that prospect sees as relevant and valuable.

Psychological Preparations

Handling Sales Negotiations require you to work in a very intensive environment with great amount of focus and attention required. This is due to the fact that a Sales Rep needs to focus on prospect requirements, objections, and proposals and at the same time delivering solutions that are viable and meets his expectations. This happens in a jiffy and your intelligent moves are all that matters. However, a little preparation would ease the way to an extent that you won't feel a pinch. So, here are few tips that you need to practice.

1. Don't be nervous before you enter the meeting.

Nervousness can kick a great amount of energy in you that can go in over enthusiasm or over consciousness making prospect believe that it is not 'your cup of tea'. You don't want that to happen. So, avoid being nervous.

2. Keeping high expectations.

A Sales Rep having great amount of expectations from the deal is vulnerable to make mistakes that can go against him in the discussion. Be a planner but don't keep expectations. You should be listening and reacting like a calm sea.

3. Be Confident.

This feeling is easy to get and sometimes hard too. It is easy to get when you feel yourself in control. But how do you feel yourself in control. A Sales Rep who is prepared for all the situations automatically feels in control and confident. So, prepare hard and you would see yourself in control. As a rule of thumb, read a little about the decision maker and always remember to start the conversation light with greetings and talking something that is not business and you will feel confident and in control.

Creating Proposal

Putting together a proposal that resonate well to the prospect is the most difficult task of all. A winning proposal is the one that has a perfect match between price and value and is convincing to a Sales Rep and his prospect. We have seen that what type of information is required to put together a winning proposal. In this section, we will see what the other important aspects of a winning proposal are and how we can get them together?

The first and foremost aspect that a prospect looks for that makes the proposal attractive is the value against the money involved. But what makes value and how you can break it down into components to be included in each of your proposals.

Adding Value Proposition

A Proposal without a value is like a body without a soul in it. A Proposal without any value in it will only get you a limited investment from the prospect restricted to the core product after negotiations – a situation similar to who gets the bigger share of the pie and most of the time it will be your prospect. This happens all the time and with every type of organization or industry. Why to lose an investment that you can earn with a little bit of effort. And the extra investment doesn't come alone. It comes with more trust for you and your company and superior customer experience that will prove beneficial in future purchases.

Let me put a typical examples of how a bad proposal looks like that will put everything in perspective.

A standard Proposal focused on core product:

This is a typical case which doesn't focus on what prospect business's unique requirements are and misses a big opportunity. A Business is looking to partner with you and apart from your key solution; they may require a good support from you to implement your solution since they lack the technical expertise but may not be aware of it till they actually face it or they may need additional consulting for migrating from competitor solution to your solution. These are some of the basic examples.

If a Sales Rep doesn't identify these opportunities and just quote the standard offering, he misses a big opportunity to raise prospect's investment. In such situation, a Prospect would negotiate hard on your standard offer and takes the bigger share of the pie. That will be a total opportunity loss for you.

How do you add value?

A Value in sales proposal comes from those components that a prospect will need to make the most out of your solution. There are many factors like: Operation Size, Technical Expertise, Current and Future Business requirements, avoiding business risks etc… that creates additional requirements that a prospect may or may not realize but an expert like you should be able to guide. In short, a value in a Sales Proposal can be distributed in following categories:

1. Core Solution Requirements

Core solution requirements are the one that is actually being discussed all the way by clients that are present in your solution and forms the "Must Have" features or advantages that you solution has to offer. This is valuable for the prospect to solve his key business challenges that he has been facing and been in conversation with you to address those through your solution. So, if a business is struggling with not finding inquiries for his business and your solution helps them to find inquiries online through your feature sets; these features forms the core business requirement for your prospect and will be included in the proposal without a doubt. This is good enough to get your prospect onboard but not enough to "expand the pie" create a win-win situation.

2. Additional supporting requirements

Additional support requirements form the value part of the proposal and help you creating a winning proposal where you demonstrate how well you understand and estimate your prospect requirement and include them in the proposal. Additional support requirements are those requirements of prospect that will add value to his business by offering Growth, Automation, Profit or avoiding loss through perceived risks of any kind from the current business setup and future requirements. ".

So, here is a business that is looking to buy your inquiry generation solution for his requirements. A Sales Rep has identified that prospect doesn't have technical expertise for the following:

a. To implement your solution.
b. To operate your solution.
c. To migrate information from his existing solution to your solution.

Bingo. You now know that how to package your proposal to make it valuable for your prospect by adding additional requirements that he needs along with the core solution but may or may not be aware of. This would help you get more investment right from your first proposal and great bit of revenue for your company.

Similarly, there are many components that are attached to your solution that a prospect might have a requirement for but may or may not realize it. A Sales Rep should be focused on assessing these requirements right from the initial discussion so these can be incorporated in the proposal to make it truly valuable for your prospect. These components are as below and should serve good for an initial solid foundation but based on your solution and industry and prospect requirements may involve additional requirements from case to case.

a. Consulting
b. Training
c. Technical Support
d. Customized Requirements
e. Additional solution requirements as upsell or cross-sell
f. Warranties

This should lay down a good solid foundation for you to get started with gathering information around these from the initial engagement and use this to build your winning proposal. Please note that while Value does form the core part of your winning proposal but there are other components that are equally important and will play a key role during proposal negotiations. These are discussed in coming sections.

Packaging Proposal

The Aim of packaging a proposal is to ensure that it holds value and transparency to an extent that it should not create confusion or trigger any questions which might result in disappointment to your prospect.

Now that you have assessed the components that add value to your proposal for your prospect which is great; next challenge would be to package your proposal – bringing together three main components and that is   Core Solution + Value + Pricing. A Prospect does understand the value of your proposal but at the end of the day, investment is equally important and hence a proposal that is priced well will be appealing to the prospect without a doubt. In this section, we will see how to package your solution to make it attractive and appealing to your prospect.

Packaging involves two key steps that a Sales Rep should carefully follow to create a winning proposal for his prospect.

   a.   Deal Pricing

Deal Pricing is the process to package all the components of the deal including the core solution, additional supporting requirements and/or cross-sell solutions and pricing them. In this regards, a Sales Rep might have to build a package from the scratch for products that are sold customized to the requirement or build upon the standard packages that company is already offering. However, in both the cases, it is equally important to price it in such a way that it is attractive and reasonable to your prospect and profitable to your own firm. Your manager will help you price the deal in small and medium businesses. For bigger corporates, they have dedicated consulting teams for deal pricing with automated tools to calculate deal pricing.

While pricing should be reasonable, it is equally important to highlight price of each individual component to maintain transparency. Also, it should be noted that precise price points are highlighted and should not include ranges like $150 - $350 for technical support per month. This hides transparency and creates confusion in prospect mind.

It is equally important to provide any calculations involved so your prospect doesn't have to break his head understanding how you reached a particular calculation. If there is no clarity in the proposal, it will only add to the frustration.

Also, in case of any discounts that are offered to the prospect as part of the proposal, you should clearly outline the regular price (before discount) and exclusive deal price (after discount) to ensure that prospect is aware he is already been awarded the discount as part of the proposal. Discounts description should also be highlighted in the proposal to ensure that prospect is aware of type of discounts or offers he is receiving.

Payment Terms and Conditions should be clearly highlighted and should be in sync with prospect purchase process. For this a Sales Rep should gather information from prospect or his accounting team to understand their purchase process and terms like how do they release payments, payment cycle etc. This should be incorporated to create payment terms and conditions which will primarily include information on

     i.   Payment Cycle
    ii.   Part Payments cycle
   iii.   Payment Mode with details like check/online etc.

      iv.   Proposal expiry date

      v.   Invoice generation process etc.

This information forms the key components of deal pricing and should be clearly communicated through your proposal. Also, a Sales Rep should review the proposal multiple times before releasing it to the prospect to understand any grey areas that might create confusion or trigger a question.

b. Multiple Packages

Creating a proposal that involves value will definitely increase the size of the pie or size of the investment. The size of the pie can further be increased by creating multiple packages of increasing value to ensure that a prospect has a choice for him. Everybody likes choices; it makes them feel in control. This psychological effect works in sales proposal also and this has been exploited by corporates of all sizes as part of their standard and customized packages offering and it really does wonder for them. So, what are its effects?

    1. A Prospect who receives multiple choices feels in control and likes it that way.

    2. Creating 3 proposals with the minimum package is matching the prospect current requirement should be ideal and will bring prospect focus on higher packages – ensuring that minimum package will be the last choice for him.

    3. A Prospect would prefer to negotiate on the higher packages instead of minimum package.

This would ensure that you are creating every opportunity to increase the size of the investment while delivering value at the same time and your prospect will recognize it. However, it is equally important that higher packages also stick to delivering value that is greater in comparison to lower packages otherwise it would be like fighting a lost battle as prospect would not even consider the higher packages.

Setting up the stage for winning

Creating packages that add value to your prospect's business requirements is great and is like a half battle won. Yes, I call it half battle won because you have created something that you know will fly among your prospect but as a sales rep you have to prepare yourself for those tricky moment when your prospect would bombard you with questions and try to negotiate hard. In this section, we are going to look at the high level of the situation outcomes and prepare for it so that a Sales Rep should be in complete control to direct the negotiations to its logical end: Win-Win situation. There are two important aspects to negotiations:

Proposal acceptance and Rejection Limits

You did your groundwork of collecting intelligence and prepared a winning proposal but negotiation from your prospect is inevitable. Getting something at a less price than published cost gives emotional satisfaction to everyone. That is how our mentality is. Everyone does it including me and it really feels like a winner. Yes, prospects would understand, agree and appreciate the value you have built for him in the proposal but at the same time, you can expect him to initiate a negotiation – it is just part of the game.

There are prospects who would understand the value you are offering and would do soft negotiations but then there are prospects who would try to negotiate hard and squeeze out as much as possible. And if you are upagainst a damgood salesormarketing guy then negotiations only gets harder.

In hard or soft negotiations, you have to understand that you cannot go below a certain commitment be it price or any items/accessories involved. And, if you have not prepared for it already, you would only end up saying "Let me check this and get back to you". The result would be delay and more negotiation calls to discuss the same thing again and again. But real Sales Leaders are prepared for almost anything. Yes, unless his prospect demands for the moon, they are prepared to handle any negotiations in one shot and get his prospect commitment. And the secret sauce to this is – Preparation.

Preparation includes identify the bottom limits of the proposal as a whole and individual components beyond which you cannot agree with the prospect or might need prior approval before you agree to it. Please note that this step would require a complete involvement of your manager to finalize the limits of the proposal. Let's take a look at an example to understand it better.

In the previous example of lead inquiry system, assuming you have prepared a proposal of

    a. $50,000 for 1 Year
    b. $90,000 for 2 years
    c. $1,25,000 for 3 years

Now, your proposal include software licenses along with 1 year premium support, 1 time online training delivered to prospect staff, 1 time consultation for migration limited to 1 day site visit. This is a basic example of a proposal.

To ensure that a negotiation ends up in bringing tangible value to both the parties and you would need to mark the following limits.

1. Expected limit: The limit of the proposal to which you would like to close the negotiations. In case of first proposal of $50,000, let's say you wish to close the deal at $48,000. This is the limit you would try to project to the prospect as lowest limit.

2. Lowest Limit: The actual lowest limit of the proposal beyond which you cannot move forward at all or at least without a prior approval. In this case, it can be $45,000.

3. Negotiable items: The items in the proposal on which you would agree to negotiate. In the above example, you might not wish to negotiate on licenses price but would be open to negotiate on Training and Consultation time deadline.

4. Negotiable Limits of individual items: This is the limit of individual items beyond which a prior approval is required.

Key points of Proposal

Following key points to be remembered when creating negotiable points of a proposal.

a. Negotiable points chosen should hold value to the prospect.

b. Limits should be decides in discussion with your manager who is in better position to guide you with the limits.

c. A Sales Rep should also note down the logical explanation for disputing or not agreeing to any of prospect's demand on the proposal or its component.

d. A Sales Rep should try to convince prospect with the logical explanation for not agreeing to anything.

e. Logical explanation should be focused on highlighting the loss involved for prospect and/or vendor if he agrees to prospect's demand.

This preparation is the key to success. This would ensure a meaningful negotiation discussion and a logical outcome that holds value to both the parties involved.

Proposal Information that matters

Have you ever got stuck up into a situation where you put across your point to the prospect during a negotiation but find it hard to justify? This is a typically situation that happens in negotiations where you need information to justify your explanation.

A Sales Leader not only needs to prepare for the explanation to justify his proposal but he also needs to prepare for the information that will add value to his explanation and help him convince his prospect. This is the last piece of the puzzle that needs to be figured out before you enter into a negotiation discussion with your prospect and/or his team. But what type of information would you need to prepare. This would entirely depend upon the queries that you expect from the prospects.

Let's take a look at some of the typically queries. This can be taken as a baseline but needs to be tuned to suit your prospects, product and industry.

1. Prospect would like to understand about your company future plans in relation to the solution.
2. He may inquire about upcoming features.
3. How your solution is upgraded, time gap between updates, solution upgrade process, technical support he may receive etc.
4. He may inquire about your customers, your biggest customers, their business and/or how your solution is being used by them.
5. He may inquire about the biggest issues your product or company has faced in the past.
6. He may inquire about your company size, your biggest target markets, revenue generated etc…

A Sales leader is always prepared to address these queries from customer convincingly to help him win prospect trust over and over again and win the deal as well.

Closing the Sale

Preparing for a winning proposal is great but what good is it if you cannot convert it into a commitment from your prospect. This is possible only and only if you can communicate its true value to your prospect and address his questions/concerns convincingly such that he can commit to you without a doubt and delay. This is possible only if you know your prospect's psychology and methods that are used by sales leaders to convince the prospect.

It is to be noted that negotiations are NOT a discussion limited to your solution. A Negotiation discussion is divided into two sections, your solution and company related information and second section being about your competitiveness in the industry. A Prospect would definitely like to compare your solution to your competitor regardless of your competitor is being in the race or not. So, you can expect questions fired by your prospects about your competition.

In the previous section, we have learnt techniques used by sales leaders to convince his prospect about his solution and company. In this section, we will try to understand different techniques that are being employed by a Sales Rep to communicate value proposition to his prospect and addressing his questions related to competitiveness of your solution and proposal.

Maintaining price and value of your proposal

On a negotiation table, a Sales Rep experiences different types of situations during negotiation discussions with his prospects. These situations while looks simple have a drastic effect on Price and

Value of your proposal if not handled properly. Let's take a look at the various situations that a Sales Rep may run into on the negotiation table.

Commoditize your proposal

A prospect is interested in discussing the final price of the proposal and starts comparing it with a competitor offering lesser price as compared to your proposal. This is the typically situation in negotiation when competitors involved are offering cheaper price than yours. A Prospect would like to do an App-to-Apple comparison even though it might not be the case and your solution might be way superior or holds better value.

How to defend it?

This is the situation where a Sales Rep would require employing a value based negotiation technique to maintain the value and price of the proposal. To handle this situation better, expert sales leaders restrict himself inquiring about the individual components and their value offered by the competitor to the prospect. This way Sales Rep would have a better chance to understand competitor proposal, identify gap based on prospect requirements that he is already aware of and prove the value of his own proposal to justify and uphold the price.

Demystify Value Proposition

You have worked very hard to build a proposal with individual components that is necessary to meet prospect's current and future requirements and together holds value for the final price he is going to pay. A Prospect may start comparing individual components of your proposal with your competitor in an effort to compare the least common denominator and get the best deal for him. This will result in demystifying your proposal overall value.

How to defend it?

This is slightly difficult situation to handle since the comparison done by the prospect for the individual components is based on the pricing and not the actual value that the piece holds in the entire proposal. On the face of the situation, a Sales Rep should be able to prove the value of individual component and he might have to again go in a direct comparison of the value of the component from competitor proposal.

However, behind the scene trust and relationship building with the prospect also plays a major role. If a sales rep is following all the activities discussed in the book, he should be able to steer through this with just discussing the value since the rapport, trust and relationship has already been built with the decision maker.

Past performance and history

Competitors would use anything and everything they hold against you on negotiation table. They may leak out any past performance or history about you to your prospect. Also, a prospect may discover something about your company over internet or through other sources. A prospect might discuss any past performance or history through an information that he might have gathered or aware of. In such cases, this will be an effort from prospect to ensure he is investing in right solution. If your prospect is aware of a history or past performance, he would also like to discuss it with you over negotiation table before he can commit and this can put you in a hot seat.

How to defend it?

This situation is hot and if mishandled can put you and your proposal on the back burner. The best possible way to handle this is be true about it and disclose all the information that will help a prospect confide in you and your company. The worst part can be if you try to defend yourself. Remember that prospect doesn't hold it as your mistake and you should not prove him wrong by defending it. You are on negotiation table because prospect is not so serious about it but would like to hear your explanation and what have your company done to avoid it. Be plain and simple about it and you would be good. Defending it would be a grave mistake.

These are typical sales negotiating situations a Sales Rep commonly come across. As a sales professional, you must be prepared to counter these tactics, primarily by planning, leveraging your relationships, and reinforcing the shared interests and value proposition you have worked so hard to develop for your prospect. Remember, you are selling a solution that will help your prospect accomplish their business objectives.

Tips for a great Negotiation Discussion

1. Don't surprise your prospect.

A Negotiation is all about meeting and exceeding your prospects requirements. It starts with offering and discussing the package that is inline with his current requirements – in the 3 packages strategy discussed above the lowest package out of three would be in line with prospect's expectation and should be discussed first.

In many situations, we have seen sales reps surprising their prospects by first discussing higher packages. This is a deal killer and totally disappoints your prospect and gives him an impression that you are being money minded and trying to extract more out of him. He would end up not taking higher offers and worst start negotiating hard on the lowest package.

The best approach is to start with discussing packages that is in line with his current needs and expected by him. From there, a Sales Rep should address his questions and demonstrate value about higher packages. This would ensure that your prospect is not taken by surprise and keeps confiding in you to understand higher packages value and take up the deal.

2. Do not make the first offer.

A Sales Rep should start the discussion by explaining about the proposal and inquiring about the questions and should defer himself from making the first offer.

3. Do not negotiate with yourself.

A Sales Rep should restrict himself after the first offer and wait for prospect counter offer. This is also a typical case when a Sales Rep pitch for an offer and when prospect doesn't display any interest, he go for second offer without understanding his prospect expectations. This is a mistake and may work against you to bring down the proposal price considerably.

4. Do not agree to prospect's counter offer readily.

In an effort to get commitment, sale rep makes this mistake of quickly reacting and agreeing to his prospect's counter offer without a delay. This exposes your desperation to get the commitment from the prospect and may go against you. The best way to handle it is, give it a thought and try to defend your original offer before accepting your prospect counter offer.

5. Make your point but do not sound harsh

There are instances when you and your prospect do not agree with each other. A Sales Rep is required to handle such situation with calmness and respectfully. All your justifications should be of substance and your prospect would definitely listen to those and this will avoid any deadlock the conversation may run into.

The Winning SALES PITCH

A Sales Pitch lives at the heart of the entire journey from the time a prospect gets engaged with the sales rep till the end of the engagement. A Sales pitch is needed at every stage and at every interaction with the prospect to build trust that you are not a sales rep instead you are his trusted advisor.

Sales Pitch is not just a statement about your product or prospect business. It is a combination of knowing your product, assessing your prospect complete requirements, demonstrations of knowledge and experience about your solution and market that collectively reflects that you are the master of your field and a trusted advisor to your prospect that he can rely on for correct guidance on solving his business challenges in the most appropriate way.

In the previous sections, we have completely understood what should be the attitude of a sales leader; different components that together make a Sales Pitch, how each stage of the sales process should be handled to make the most out it. However, the most crucial part of the subject is "how to package this knowledge and deliver it to your prospect" such that he feels connected and engaged all the time.

In this section, we will take a look at how to build your sales pitch that would help you demonstrate how well you understand prospect business and his challenges, competitive space and help build a solution for your prospect that will not only solve his business challenge but more than that will add value to his business for long term gains. This section is completely dedicated to how you can encapsulate all that you have learnt so far into statements that will help you get through to winning all types of accounts. This is a major challenge for any Sales Rep and I am going to discuss the practical approach to overcome this challenge easily.

This specific approach has been designed after thorough study of sales rep challenges and experimentation keeping in mind:

a. Knowledge gap that exists between your prospect and you when he first contacts you.

b. Limited time available to Sales Rep to bring his prospect up to the speed with regards to solution.

c. Vast amount of knowledge that needs to be shared with prospect in limited time while maintaining his interest.

This Approach focuses on delivering:

a. Establishing a quick platform for knowledge sharing that is in sync with prospect interest and requirements.

b. Information sharing is precise in terms of time taken to share the information.

c. Information is limited in words but high in value and tuned to prospect requirements.

To understand this most effective and practical approach, we need to first understand critical components related to it.

Sales Decision Curve

Every solution or service purchase requires a prospect to make decisions at different stages of the Sales Funnel. It starts with choosing a vendor to engage with for his requirements and goes on from there till a solution is selected and purchased. A Sales

Rep responsibility is to equip himself with all the details and communicate it to his prospect in such a way that helps him with effective decision making. So, to understand what are those decisions and how an effective sales leader can help his prospect steer through; we would first need to understand the "Decision Curve" that prospects needs to follow.

Viability

This is the most crucial phase of the decision curve as prospect exist in the top layer of the sales funnel i.e. "Prospecting & Qualification" and in the mode of assessing the viability of your solution to decide if he would like to purse this solution and invest his resources further. Since, this decision going to cost him a lot more than just time, a prospect needs more than right information to make a call to continue further. The right information includes product benefits, cost, support structure, brand authority etc... provided in a concise and clear manner that will help him assess the viability of your solution for his own requirements.

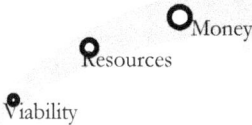

Resources

This is the second phase of the decision curve. In this stage, a prospect requires to put your solution to evaluation. From a prospect perspective, it would require him to allocate dedicated human resources based on solution and scale of operation, time & energy, other IT & Non-IT resources based on the type of solutions and services which definitely is a cost to a business –

direct cost or opportunity cost. Opportunity cost is the loss of other alternatives when one alternative is chosen.

Since, there is a direct and indirect cost involved for a prospect, he needs to make an important call to continue with the proposal or not. Hence, he requires lot more deeper details through a meeting or presentation about product technical, physical, economical aspects along with brand authority of your company. Hence, it is quite crucial for a sales rep to ensure the details offered to him are good enough for a positive decision to move along the decision curve and down the sales funnel.

Money

This is the final stage of the Pre-Sales funnel where a prospect/company decides to come in relation with other company like a marriage by purchasing his product. So, a prospect has to take a call if and when to purchase the solution and how much to invest initially during the first purchase. Also, how to get the maximum benefit from the deal would be his priorities. This is an important call to make as a prospect has come a long way and moving forward would mean a relationship of couple of years at least and backing off from here and pursuing another solution would mean a double direct and opportunity cost to him.

So, a sales rep holds the responsibility to establish his brand trust and proves his solution viability for prospect's requirements again with the required details.

Hence, telling about your product involves much more than just knowing the product details.

Decision curve challenge

Sales Reps holds a bigger responsibility of helping prospects steer through the decision curve. This makes it so much important to convey the details. However, it is equally important to know how to share details to convince the prospect and makes it easier for him to take a call. But sharing the Same Technical, Physical, Economical aspects of your solution in the same manner aren't going to help a sales rep at all. Initial stage of decision curve requires a sales rep to share more details in concise manner to help prospect understand key points about the proposal and decide on proposal viability whereas second stage of decision curve require sales rep to share same information in greater details addressing the need of wider audience like IT/Non-IT decision makers. This further complicates the matter. So, it is quite important for a sales rep to understand the challenges posed by decision making curve for a sales rep before we take a look at the solution.

Depth of details

A decision curve requires a sales rep to help support his prospect decision by offering him required details. However, sharing same details isn't of much help like in the beginning stage of the interaction, a prospect requires concise details like type of features and benefits offered by the solution whereas during evaluation of solution a prospect would require in-depth details of features like its functionality etc…

Hence, a Sales Rep should know each product feature, its benefit and application in depth.

Need of Wider details

A Sales rep is expected to help prospects with all the details he require during his decision making curve to support the concept of "Single-Point-of Contact". Regardless of the complexity of the solution, a prospect expects to maintain a one point of contact and look up to his sales rep to be the lead runner and help him with details and decision making. This requires a sales rep to help his prospect understanding not only technical aspect of the solution but also with Physical, Economical and in many cases Social Aspect of the solution along with helping with the details related to customer base, company culture, competitive analysis and lot more.

Now, this poses a greater challenge for sales rep as they have to be on toes to help prospects with details and always running short of time and has to face monstrous curiosity of prospects to get the details as soon as possible.

Need of Wider Audience

Sales Trends have changed. With the last recession this planet has seen, one important change the sales world has seen is the involvement of multiple decision makers even in the simplest of solutions sale – as simple as a shampoo which now involves 2 decision makers' husband and wife. Complex solutions like Software, heavy machinery involves multiple decision makers across all horizontals (Sales, marketing, Accounts, ITetc) and verticals (Top Management, Middle Management etc…) of a company.

This requires a Sales Rep to not only know all the details about his solution but also the art to prioritize the details based on the decision makers profile. For example, a CEO might be interested in economical aspect of the solution whereas IT head is looking for high level techno-economic aspects of the details whereas a technical assistant might only be interested in its IT dependencies.

This requires a sales rep to not only know the details but also to know how to position the details. This further poses a challenge to remember more details and knowing how to prioritize and position them along the decision curve based on the audience involved.

How the winning sales pitch works

Get a grip on details that matters

Sales industry is undergoing a shift. A shift from Filed Sales to Inside Sales; this has been the trend in the last few years and will continue to be the trend going forward. And with the growing competition, every company now is looking to enhance a prospect experience by reducing the gap to information as much as possible. But how's that possible. The only way it is possible to equip your sales team to be true sales leaders that are ready to handle any information request with the speed of the light. Being into Sales for over a decade, I have always felt it and now it has turned into a primary tool to engage the prospect and win over the competition.

Well, that would be a tough situation for a sales rep to get a grip around all the details in a way to address all types of needs of all types of decision maker.

This was a challenge for me as well and the sales team that I had built or handled all the way till I discovered this approach. This has been the secret sauce of success in engaging and winning clients and accounts of all types and sizes by all members of my team with minimum efforts. This approach is applicable to all type of sales and all types of accounts a Sales Rep is involved in like:

    a.   Consumer or Business,
    b.   Small, Mid or High Value accounts,
    c.   Complex or Simple Solution accounts,
    d.   Domestic or International accounts, you just name it.

Organize the Intel

So, how does it work? Well, just like a book has an index in the beginning to highlight the content of the book, for every product or solution I or my team has been involved in selling, I used to create index for that product. An index that would only include the highlights or key points about the solutions

    a.   Technical Aspect
    b.   Economical Aspect
    c.   Social Aspect
    d.   Prospect business aspect
    e.   Competitive aspect

Now, each section would include sub-sections which would be prospects challenges based on the prospect's profiling. Further, it will include solutions features and benefits supporting the challenges. Solution Benefits will highlight 3 key points for each of the key decision maker.

This was repeated for each section I have highlighted above. Thereafter, I practiced the elaboration part. For each point, I wrote few sentences including key benefits and functionality that would help me memorize and remember the things to talk about if I need to elaborate.

I then wrote this on paper and stuck it up on my desk and follow the pattern on every call. After couple of weeks and few hundreds of calls and presentations, I no longer needed the paper and that was it.

Now, one thing to highlight here is that I have avoided any big lines or big paragraphs. My index only included one key word related to the section or sub section in question. When I was done; for majority of the product, I had about 25 to 50 lines or words to remember that summarized my entire solution for all types of key decision makers.

Become a winner

Self-Prepared

What good this can do to you? Well, I got the taste of its success in every type of interaction I had with prospect regardless of the channel or occasion I was in, I was all prepared. For example, for prospecting over phone, I used to only highlight the key challenges and features and other things without elaborating anything and without missing anything. In presentations, I used to follow the same pattern but this time I used to highlight and elaborate as much as needed. In conferences where I am up for networking, I just used to give a taste of very few key points and sub points and in public speaking, I used to prioritize it accordingly and speak. So, I was all prepared for any type of interactions without feeling nervous and without missing any key details.

Team Training

The story doesn't end here. It has further more benefits like, when building sales team and training them, I could reduce their training time from months to weeks that were like 50% reduction in training time. In fact, newly hired sales reps were on the job and started producing within 2 months as opposed to 6 months' time frame before. And to count the benefit to them, they were equipped to handle any and all type of interactions on their own without involving a supervisor – end-to-end in just 3 to 4 months. Can you believe that? So, it was not only useful to turn myself on the path of a sales leader but it was also useful to train and get the teams ready.

Thought Leadership

By definition, a thought leader refers to an individual or firm that is recognized as an authority in a specialized field and whose expertise is sought and often rewarded. However, colloquially, this includes producing content over a specific topic through digital and physical channels like blogs, whitepapers, eBooks, books etc… This attracts readers connect with the content creator, trust him and establish relationship with him.

Content has changed the way businesses work. With internet, every business is online. And with thought leadership, every business is trying to get their prospect's attention. Businesses are producing every type of content they can to help their prospects make smart decisions. On the other end, prospects who wish to buy products, get onto internet; consume as much information as they can before they contact vendors. By the time they contact the vendor, they are already aware of your solution.

This has changed the way sales are done now where prospect is in complete control of interactions and not the vendors. Prospects browse and reads about your solution, about your company and position it accordingly which has a great influence on his engagement with the sales rep. Sales Rep would be in the show if the information available to prospect is quality information whereas a Sales Rep would have tough time convincing a prospect if the first impression is not good due to lack of information or lack of quality information.

In this section, we will learn about how Sales Rep can tap the potential of Thought Leadership for better and higher conversions.

Thought Leadership for Sales Professionals

A Sales Rep core responsibility is to lead customer engagement and convert accounts. In today's virtual world, outside of retail and e-commerce world, no deals are signed without a sales rep involved and guiding a prospect through his decision curve. For Sales Rep, ability to lead the prospect is must. But top sales leaders have already realized that being a true sales leader extend beyond the limits of leading. They have already realized the role of Thought Leadership in lead engagement and conversion and have exploited its potential fully to crack on the mid and large size accounts. Hence, the notion of establishing Thought Leadership has emerged as a top priority for sales and marketing success.

So, what's the deal with content? Content is simply the King. Content has become the lifeline of every business decision. We are driven by content – our discussions, our decisions are all driven by the content. Great content tie us together and help establishes a relationship between the content creator and reader whereas bad or boring content disappoint and creates a bad image. In any ways, content plays a huge role in our life.

This indeed is a great challenge for a Sales Rep to handle prospects assumption which may be positive or negative. It also presents a great opportunity for Sales Professionals to come out and tap the true potential of Thought Leadership to establish trust and relationship with his prospect even before they establish a contact. This is achieved by taking part in thought leadership. So, let us see the benefits it brings to the table for a Sales Professional and how to tap its potential to establish yourself as a Sales Leader.

Prospect Trust

Thought Leadership helps you build trust with your prospects based on the principal of likeability to Familiarity and then to Trust.

So, you have read an article written by some X person and you liked it a lot. You have just developed a favorable positioning about the person. Next is you speak to him, you feel a sense of familiarity & comfort when talking to him. You also start to trust him. This happens to me all the time. Does it happen to you as well? Congrats, you have just witnessed the power of "Thought Leadership".

That is how we are. We confide, trust in someone or at the least feel comfortable with who we already know or have heard of. If we like their piece of work, our trust just increases without a doubt. This works in the favor of a Sales Professional who is into Thought leadership. They always holds an upper hand with prospects that like and trust them before even contacting them and the result is - your efforts to get your prospect's trust has just reduced to half and chances of converting the account just got doubled. That is the power of "Thought Leadership".

How does it benefit you?

Thought Leadership plays crucial role at two different important stages of the sales process.

Building Prospect Trust

With the advent of internet and social media, a sales process has completely changed to the effect that a prospect studies a brand first and it's offering before contacting it. Information provided by organizations over internet/website serves the purpose. Information produced by Sales Rep helps builds the trust with the

prospect such that he is already aware of his work and developed familiarity and likeability for him. This helps convert his likeability into trust quickly and works to the sales rep advantage.

Engaging Prospect Better

Sales deal closing happens through information sharing at multiple stages to engage the prospect during solution introduction, trial and closing. A Sales Rep involved in thought leadership can proactively share blogs, articles and white papers produced by him for his product or prospect business requirements will help him engage prospect better, add value at every stage by proactively sharing information that is useful to the prospect and strengthen the relation they share further.

This also gives opportunity to Sales Rep to reduce their inactive or dead accounts in their pipeline by sharing information with prospects that holds value for them instead of poking them with boring standard templates which are of no use to them. Prospects would like information that offers value to them, would maintain touch with you and trust you. This will ultimately reduce your inactive and dead accounts.

In essence, this activity not only help you develop trust with your prospect but also reduces your sales cycle as prospect who trust you walk along with you through the decision curve a lot quicker when compared to normal process. This will ensure your sales cycle period is decreasing. As per recent surveys, sales leaders have witnessed an increase is prospect spending on his first order where sales leaders involved are into thought leadership.

This opportunity is what separating a Sales leader from a Sales Rep. A Sales Leader uses it as a tool to get prospect trust and convert better and bigger.

Appreciation and Growth

A Sales Rep involved in thought leadership not only see bigger and better conversions from prospects but have far reaching benefits within the organization as well. While there are many tangible and non-tangible benefits associated with the "Thought Leadership", I would like to highlight the benefits that are tangible and directly impact your growth and personal brand within the organization.

Meeting and Exceeding Quotas

A Sales Rep constantly producing high quality content focused on his prospects will result in engaging and converting more accounts. At the same time, Thought Leadership results in converting accounts at a lesser period of time. This ensure that a Sales Rep not only convert more accounts at a higher ticket size but at the same time convert accounts in lesser period of time which will positively impact his pipeline.

More conversions at higher investments with less efforts and time will help him meet and exceed his quotas beyond the expectations. This will result in earning him more incentives per account. More commissions' results in more urge to do better and always keep his motivation high.

Expert Positioning

Expert positioning is all about proving that you are the best at it. A Sales Rep who meets and exceed his quotas beyond expectations. Publish his experiences, advise, researches related information through articles and white papers seen as an expert in his domain and that is "Thought Leadership" all about – being seen as an expert in your area. This is the first immediate change that a Sales Rep involved in thought leadership would experience. Thought Leadership in the area of sales is mostly handled by Sales Experts and Leaders and if you are doing it - you are ensuring that you are seen as one of them. This will eventually position you as an expert internally and will have a direct impact on your growth within the organization.

Customers Appreciations

Customer Appreciations are related to Customer Experience he has had with you and your organization. Yes, great Customer Service results in great Customer Experience and great Customer Experience converts in Customer Appreciation. Customer Appreciation is rare these days and the only reason for that is great Customer Service.

A Prospect who is engaged with a Sales Rep who is seen as an expert through Thought Leadership he is involved in. He has helped his prospect understand the solution, company, competitive space with the quality of information he shared face to face and through thought leadership. This is basis of a great customer experience and a prospect that experience the great customer service will never forget or hesitate to reward you with order and appreciation.

These appreciations from prospects and customers will add to your creditability and your expert positioning among the organization.

Marketing

Thought Leadership benefits are not just limited to sales professional individual benefits but it extends to marketing and overall firm brand reputation thus strengthening your personal brand as a Sales Professional. We have discussed these benefits below:

Search Engine Ranking

Search Engine Ranking is a marketing activity where every organization would like to be ranked on top by every prominent search engine like Google, Bing and Yahoo. As you might be aware of these search engines are the major sources of organic traffic to any website. A Prospect searches for a solution using keywords based on his requirements. Search engines based on the keywords typed by searcher, pulls up results that best matches prospect query and displays it on their pages top results being displayed first.

Now, every organization would like to be on 1st page of search engine as prospects select vendors from the first page of search engine. This brings in additional inquiries for an organization that converts into more qualified inquires and more revenue. To be on the first page, an organization uses "Thought Leadership" to produce lot of quality content regularly that is full of keywords and help search engine index it and pop it up based on search queries of prospects.

A Sales Rep involved in "Thought Leadership" producing great quality content will be helping its marketing team generate more quality inquiries online. A Marketing Team benefiting from its Sales Teams efforts will recognize the efforts and surely the efforts will help establishing your positing and contribution in your marketing team and company success.

Reviving dead and inactive accounts

In a marketing and sales process, typically dead and inactive accounts are handled by the marketing team on a bulk level.

Marketing team is also tasked with the responsibility of reviving these accounts and converting them in a qualified inquiry. Marketing team uses various email and social media campaigns to share information generated through "Thought Leadership" to revive these types of accounts.

Articles generated by Sales Team that is quality rich out of their experience plays a great role in reviving such accounts. Hence, a Sales Professional makes a great contribution in this area of marketing as well to ensure they are successful.

Other benefits

As you have noticed already the monstrous role "Thought Leadership" plays in your individual success within the organization as well as your company success. This is the single most reason a Sales Rep can dive into "Thought Leadership" to become a true sales leader. However, the benefits don't end. Yes, you must be wondering what's next.

A Sales Rep involved in "Thought Leadership" is widely recognized in the industry and this also helps proves his creditability to other organizations which really does wonders when he is applying for job in other organizations. With the advent of Social Media, organizations recruiting process has completely changed and they look for candidate creditability over social media and internet before even calling him for the interview. A candidate that has widely recognized creditability over social media and his company website through "Thought Leadership" is already a winner without a doubt. This also helps other organization reach to conclusions very quickly about candidate hiring and turns out to be a win-win situation for both of them.

Types of Content

For those who are not already into it, I am sure; I already got your interest in "Thought Leadership" with its far reaching benefits and humungous role in meeting your aspiring career goals and success. And, you must be wondering what type of content regarded as successful and how can I get started with it.

"Thought Leadership" is all about quality content. Did you notice the word "quality"? Yes, quality is the one that makes content worth reading. If an article is without quality – it is as good as dead. No one would be interested in reading it. Hence, you should be focusing your energy on producing quality content for your readers. Readers get to read quality content and you get their appreciation. So, what makes a content quality content?

Here I am listing the ingredient that makes a quality content.

Important Advise: It is a great idea to connect with your marketing team to understand the type of content that resonate well among your target audience. This is a tactical decision and marketing team is expert to guide you on the type of content that your prospects will prefer.

What is the ultimate aim of the content; to resolve someone problem? A piece of content that resolves problems or provide answers is a great piece of content. People gets online to get their questions answered, queries clarified and problems solved. These questions, queries or problems may relate to their business or personal interest. Hence, articles focused on business and personal interests make a great piece of content.

For a Sales Professional who is looking to establish himself as a "Thought Leader" to earn prospect trust can start with focusing on these areas:

Solution features and benefits

A Sales Rep everyday interact with many prospects who inquire about many different types of features and situations that they would like to resolve with your solution. Hence, it would be a great idea to capture this information and publish it online to address questions and concerns prospects have around it.

Business Challenges

A Prospect shares a lot of information with Sales Rep regarding his requirements and business challenges. Each prospect is unique, their requirements are unique and their challenges are unique. Hence, this creates a great opportunity for a Sales Rep to capture this information and build content around it that addresses these challenges. This would require you to map it with your solution benefits and how your solution benefits address these challenges. Makes a great piece of content totally focused on prospect business challenges.

Solution competitiveness

A Prospect is always curious to learn about your solution and brand competitiveness to understand the value he will receive by partnering with your brand. This offers a great opportunity for a Sales Rep to publish content around your solution and brand competitiveness and how uniquely you are placed in the market as compared to your competition. It offers your prospect a great way to clarify their doubts and an edge to you over your competition.

Value Proposition

With the ever growing competition, it is not possible for a brand now to strictly compete on the solution alone. Customer Service and other benefits do count a lot and prospects are very curious to understand your value proposition when partnering with you. A Sales Rep can grab this opportunity to write about the unique value proposition that your brand has to offer to your prospects which makes you a great partner for them. Prospects will like it as it makes a great piece of content for them.

Case Studies and Success Stories

What else can be a great piece of content for your prospects than learning about how your existing customers are using your solutions and how they have been successful with it? A Prospect is going to invest in your solution and in big ticket deals where millions of dollars are involved this is a must. So, if you can give your prospect success stories of your existing customers then making decision for him about your solution becomes far easier. You have just solved his biggest problem and he would make sure to reward you for this.

Industry News & Trends

Everyone is news hungry. Everyone wants to stay on top of the industry news and trends for effective decision making. This is especially true for people in the top management who are responsible for making organization wide strategy and policy and in most cases are your target decision makers. Staying on top of the industry trends and news that will be relevant to your prospect and sharing it with them makes a great piece of content. This also ensures that you always have a piece or two to talk about to your prospect out of your solution discussion.

Content Format

If quality content is the soul of "Thought Leadership" then content format makes the body of it. How do you package and display your content is equally important. A Prospect gets your piece of content in multiple formats like Blogs, Videos, White Papers, eBooks etc...

These are the common formats that are used by prospects to digest the information. A Sales Rep can produce content in any of these formats. However, before you can produce content in any of your favorite format, it is highly important to take your marketing team advise to understand what is the most favorite content format that your target audience is using to digest the information. This is a tactical move and would require the involvement of the marketing team as they are the expert in the matter to suggest the format that resonates well among your audience. Hence, it is highly recommended to involve marketing team before a decision is taken by you on this. With this in mind, let us take a look at the various formats and their features.

Blogs

Blogs are a short piece of content 1 page (500 to 2,000 words) that discusses a particular problem or question in details. It is focused on one component like a solution feature or a prospect/customer situation related to a feature or two. A blog is commonly available on your website as a separate page. Blogs are published online in various categories and shared with prospects across all types of channels like website, email, social media etc…

Blogs are very common now a days and a very good way for prospects to figure out multiple things about your company like, solution features, how serious are your about content publishing, how actively you have been publishing content and how engaged is your audience.

eBook

eBooks are a long piece of content ranging from 10 pages to 100 pages depending upon how deep you would like your topic to be. eBooks have become very popular in Social Media Age for various reasons.

eBooks are a long piece of content. It covers a topic in details. They are difficult to prepare and requires a lot of efforts in terms of writing the content as well as presenting it well. It typically takes from couple of weeks to couple of months to produce a eBook for an individual or organization.

Infographics

Infographics is a visual representation of information or data. This includes representation of information through lot of pictures and minimal text. Infographics are regarded as a short piece of content since it ranges from 3 to 10 pages typically. Infographics are a highly focused piece of content and very simple to read and understand. However, it takes a lot of efforts to write the content since most of them is pictures and its representation is highly critical.

Infographics have become very popular due its simplicity to consume the content and other being its intuitiveness. Readers find it lot simple to consume the content as it hardly takes about few minutes to consume the content and it is very simple to consume as it is mostly loaded with pictures.

I hope you have enjoyed the journey to becoming a Sales Leader and get benefitted from the real world and practical advises provided in the book.

Remember:
People buy into the leader before they buy into their vision. — John Maxwell

Sales Plan & Presentations Chart

Battles are won with Swords and Guns. An efficient Sales Leader needs effective tools to achieve a performance that cannot be matched. To download free 'SALES PLAN' and 'PRESENTATION CHART", visit our Facebook page.

Dishah keeps producing free and paid sales resources that include activities, tools, knowledge sharing videos that proves to be very effective for Sales Reps in staying ahead at every step. To download free resources, please visit our facebook page:

www.facebook.com/dishahco

To stay on top of latest sales trends, sales news, winning sales strategies that will help you stay head, please visit and subscribe for our blog page here,

www.dishahconsultants.com/blog.php

For receiving Sales related updates, training videos and session on twitter, please visit

@dishahco

If you are on Google+ and would like to be connected and updated on sales trends and news, please follow us on:

https://plus.google.com/+DishahStrategicSolutionsPvtLtd/posts

If you would like to leave a word to the 'author' of the book, you can communicate your feedback directly to him using the link https://in.linkedin.com/in/amitsharma04.

www.ingramcontent.com/pod-product-compliance
Lightning Source LLC
Chambersburg PA
CBHW060443040426

42331CB00044B/2514